BRIAN CLARK was born in 1932 and was educated in Bristol, England, and at the Central School of Speech and Drama, and the University of Nottingham. He taught in schools for eight years and was Staff Tutor in Drama at the University of Hull from 1968 to 1972. *Whose Life Is It Anyway?*, originally televised in 1972, was Mr. Clark's first professional production. Since then he has written over twenty television plays. His work for the stage includes collaboration on *Lay By* and *England's Ireland* for the Portable Theatre and two plays for the Soho Poly, London—*Post Mortem* and *Campion's Interview*.

WHOSE LIFE IS IT ANYWAY?

BRIAN CLARK

 A BARD BOOK/PUBLISHED BY AVON BOOKS

CAUTION: Professionals and amateurs are hereby warned that WHOSE LIFE IS IT ANYWAY?, being protected under the Copyright Laws of the United States of America, the British Commonwealth, including the Dominion of Canada, and all other countries of the International Copyright Union and the Universal Copyright Convention, is subject to royalty. All rights, including professional, amateur, motion picture, recitation, lecturing, public reading, radio and television broadcasting, and the rights of translation into foreign languages, are strictly reserved. Particular emphasis is laid on the question of readings, permission for which must be obtained from the author's agent in writing. Amateur groups must secure such permission from The Dramatic Publishing Company at 4150 N. Milwaukee Ave., Chicago, Illinois 60641 and stock and repertoire groups must secure permission from Samuel French Ltd. at 25 W. 45th St., New York, N.Y. All other permissions must be secured by Judy Daish Associates Ltd., Globe Theatre, Shaftesbury Ave., London W1V7AA, England.

Cover art from the original Broadway show-poster. Design by Frank "Fraver" Verlizzo.

AVON BOOKS
A division of
The Hearst Corporation
959 Eighth Avenue
New York, New York 10019

Copyright © 1978 by Brian Clark
Published by arrangement with Dodd, Mead & Company
Library of Congress Catalog Card Number: 79-16470
ISBN: 0-380-52407-4

All rights reserved, which includes the right to reproduce this book or portions thereof in any form whatsoever. For information address Dodd, Mead and Company, 79 Madison Avenue, New York, New York 10016

First Bard Printing, November, 1980

BARD IS A TRADEMARK OF THE HEARST CORPORATION AND IS REGISTERED IN MANY COUNTRIES AROUND THE WORLD, MARCA REGISTRADA, HECHO EN U.S.A.

Printed in the U.S.A.

For Maggie

The first television performance of WHOSE LIFE IS IT ANYWAY? *was transmitted on March 12, 1972, by Granada TV. It was produced by Peter Eckersley and directed by Richard Everitt, with Ian McShane as Ken, Susanne Neve as Dr. Scott and Philip Latham as Dr. Emerson.*

The first stage performance was given at the Mermaid Theatre, London, in association with Ray Cooney Limited on March 6, 1978. It was directed by Michael Lindsay-Hogg and designed by Alan Tagg, with the following cast:

KEN HARRISON	*Tom Conti*
SISTER ANDERSON	*Jennie Goossens*
KAY SADLER	*Phoebe Nicholls*
JOHN	*Trevor Thomas*
DR. SCOTT	*Jane Asher*
DR. EMERSON	*Richard Leech*
MRS. BOYLE	*Rona Anderson*
PHILIP HILL	*Richard Ireson*
DR. PAUL TRAVERS	*Edward Lyon*
PETER KERSHAW	*Alan Brown*
DR. BARR	*Peter Honri*
ANDREW EDEN	*Robert Gary*
MR. JUSTICE MILLHOUSE	*Sebastian Shaw*

The first New York stage performance was presented by Emanuel Azenberg, James M. Nederlander and Ray Cooney, by arrangement with Mermaid Theatre Trust, at the Trafalgar Theatre on April 17, 1979. It was directed by Michael Lindsay-Hogg and designed by Alan Tagg, with the following cast:

KEN HARRISON	*Tom Conti*
SISTER ANDERSON	*Beverly May*
KAY SADLER	*Pippa Pearthree*
JOHN	*Damien Leake*
DR. SCOTT	*Jean Marsh*
DR. EMERSON	*Philip Bosco*
MRS. BOYLE	*Veronica Castang*
PHILIP HILL	*Kenneth Welsh*
DR. PAUL TRAVERS	*Peter McRobbie*
PETER KERSHAW	*Russell Leib*
DR. BARR	*Edmond Genest*
ANDREW EDEN	*Richard de Fabees*
MR. JUSTICE MILLHOUSE	*James Higgins*

Characters in order of appearance

KEN HARRISON	*The Patient*
SISTER ANDERSON	*Ward Sister (Supervisor)*
NURSE KAY SADLER	*A Probationer Nurse*
JOHN	*A West Indian Ward Orderly*
DR. CLARE SCOTT	*Junior Registrar*
DR. MICHAEL EMERSON	*Consultant Physician*
MRS. GILLIAN BOYLE	*A Medical Social Worker*
PHILIP HILL	*Ken's Solicitor*
DR. PAUL TRAVERS	*Consultant Psychiatrist*
PETER KERSHAW	*Ken's Barrister*
DR. BARR	*Consultant Psychiatrist (from Norwood Park Hospital)*
ANDREW EDEN	*Hospital's Barrister*
MR. JUSTICE MILLHOUSE	*Judge*

The action is continuous and takes place in a side ward, offices, corridors and a road outside a general hospital.

WHOSE LIFE IS IT ANYWAY?

ACT ONE

(SISTER ANDERSON *and* NURSE KAY SADLER
enter with trolley)

SISTER

Good morning, Mr. Harrison. A new face for you
today.

KEN

That's nice.

NURSE

Hello.

KEN

Hello. I'm afraid I can't offer you my hand. You'll
just have to make do with my backside like all the
other nurses.
    (*They lower the bed*)
Going down—Obstetrics, Gynecology, Lingerie,
Rubber wear.
    (*They roll* KEN *over and start to massage
    his back and heels with spirit and talc*)

1

It's funny, you know. I used to dream of situations like this.

SISTER
Being injured?

KEN
No! Lying on a bed being massaged by two beautiful women.

SISTER
(*Mock serious*)
If you go on like this, Mr. Harrison, I shan't be able to send my young nurses in here.

KEN
They're perfectly safe with me, Sister.
(*The phone rings outside*)

SISTER
Can you manage for a moment, Nurse?

NURSE
Oh, yes, Sister.

SISTER
Wipe your hands and put the pillows behind Mr. Harrison; we don't want to have him on the floor.

KEN
Have me on the floor, Sister, please. Have me on the floor.

(SISTER *goes out*)

What's your name?

NURSE

Kay.

KEN

That's nice, but don't let Sister hear you say that.

NURSE

What?

KEN

What's your second name?

NURSE

Sadler.

KEN

Then you must answer "Nurse Sadler" with a smile
that is full of warmth, but with no hint of sex.

NURSE

I'm sorry.

KEN

I'm not. I'm glad you're called Kay. I shall call you
Kay when we're alone, just you and me, having my
backside caressed . . .

NURSE

I'm rubbing your heels.

KEN

Well, don't spoil it. After all, it doesn't matter. I can't feel anything wherever you are. Is this your first ward?

NURSE

Yes. I'm still at P.T.S.

KEN

What's that? Primary Training School?

NURSE

Yes. I finish next week.

KEN

And you can't wait to get here full time.

NURSE

I'll be glad to finish the school.

KEN

All students are the same.

NURSE

Were you a teacher?

KEN

Tut tut; second lesson. You mustn't use the past tense.

NURSE

What do you mean?

KEN

You said: "Were you a teacher?" You should have
said: "Are you a teacher?" I mean, you are now part
of the optimism industry. Everyone who deals with
me acts as though, for the first time in the history of
medical science, a ruptured spinal column will heal
itself—it's just a bit of a bore waiting for it to happen.

NURSE

I'm sorry.

KEN

Don't be. Kay, you're a breath of fresh air.
              (SISTER *comes back*)

SISTER

Finished, Nurse?

KEN

What do you mean? Have I finished Nurse. I
haven't started her yet!

NURSE

Yes, Sister.
              (*They roll him back and remake the bed*)

KEN

I must congratulate you, Sister, on your new recruit.
A credit to the monstrous regiment.

SISTER

I'm glad you got on.

KEN

Well, I didn't get quite that far. Not that I didn't try, Sister. But all I could get out of her was that her name was . . . Nurse Sadler . . . and that she's looking forward to coming here.

SISTER

If she still feels like that after being five minutes with you, we'll make a nurse of her yet.

KEN

I don't know quite how to take that Sister—lying down I suppose.

SISTER

Night Sister said you slept well.

KEN

Ah-thew. I fooled her . . . After her last round, a mate of mine came in and smuggled me out . . . We went midnight skateboarding.

SISTER

Oh yes . . . I hope it was fun . . .

KEN

It was all right . . . The only problem was that I was the skateboard.

SISTER

There, that's better. Comfortable?

KEN

Sister, it's so beautifully made, I can't feel a thing.

SISTER

Cheerio, Mr. Harrison

          (They leave)

NURSE

Won't he ever get better, Sister?

SISTER

No.

NURSE

What will happen to him?

SISTER

When we have him fully stabilized, he'll be transferred to a long-stay hospital.

NURSE

For the rest of his life?

SISTER

Yes.

          (JOHN, *an orderly, comes along the corridor carrying shaving tackle on a tray*)

JOHN

Morning, Sister.

SISTER

Morning, John. Are you going to Mr. Harrison?

JOHN

That's right.

SISTER

He's all ready.

JOHN

Right.
>   (JOHN *goes into the sluice room to collect*
>   *an electric razor*)

NURSE

How long has he been here?

SISTER

Four months.

NURSE

How much longer will he be here?

SISTER

Not much longer now, I should think. Take the trolley into the ward, Nurse. I should start on Mr. Phil-
lips.
>   (SISTER *goes into her office.* JOHN *goes into*
>   KEN's *room. He plugs in the razor and*
>   *shaves* KEN)

JOHN

Good morning, Mr. Harrison . . .

KEN

Come to trim the lawn?

JOHN

That's right.

KEN

Good . . . Must make sure that all the beds and borders are neat and tidy.

JOHN

That's my job.

KEN

Well, my gardening friend, isn't it about time you got some fertilizer to sprinkle on me and get some movement going in this plant?

JOHN

Ah, now there you have me. You see, I'm only a laborer in this here vineyard. Fertilizers and pruning and bedding out is up to the head gardener.

KEN

Still, you must be in charge of the compost heap. That's where I should be.

(SISTER *puts her head around the door*)

SISTER

John.

JOHN

Yes?

SISTER

Don't be long, will you. Dr. Scott will probably be early today; there's a consultant's round this morning.

JOHN

Right, Sister.

> (SISTER *goes back to her office*)

KEN

The visitation of the Gods.

JOHN

Eh?

KEN

The Gods are walking on earth again.

JOHN

Oh yes—they think they're a bit of all right.

KEN

What happened to the other chap—Terence, he was called . . . I think?

JOHN

They come and they go . . . I think he left to get married up north somewhere.

KEN

Terence, getting married? Who to? A lorry driver?

JOHN

Catty!

KEN

No. Bloody jealous. From where I'm lying, if you can make it at all—even with your right hand—it

would be heaven . . . I'm sorry . . . feeling sorry
for myself this morning . . . I can't even say I got
out of the wrong side of the bed. Are you down to
the bone yet? . . . Anyway, how long will you be
staying?

JOHN

Just till we go professional, man.

KEN

Doing what?

JOHN

Music. We got a steel band—with some comedy
numbers and we're getting around a bit . . . We're
auditioning for Opportunity Knocks in four months.

KEN

That's great . . . Really great . . . I like steel
bands . . . There's something fascinating about
using oil drums—making something out of
scrap . . . Why not try knocking a tune out of me?

JOHN

Why not, man!
(He puts down his razor and, striking KEN
*very lightly up and down his body like a
xylophone, sings a typical steel band tune,
moving rhythmically to the music.* KEN *is
delighted.* DR. CLARE SCOTT *comes in.*
JOHN *stops)*

DR. SCOTT

Don't stop . . .

JOHN

It's all right . . . I've nearly finished.
   (*He makes one more pass with the razor*)

KEN

I was just making myself beautiful for you, Doctor.

JOHN

There . . . Finished.
     (*He goes to the door*)

KEN

Work out some new tunes . . . Hey, if Doctor Scott
could drill some holes in my head, you could blow
in my ear and play me like an ocarina.

JOHN

I'll see you later.
    (*He grins and goes out*)

DR. SCOTT

You're bright and chirpy this morning.

KEN
(*Ironically*)

It's marvelous, you know. The courage of the
human spirit.

DR. SCOTT
(*Dryly*)

Nice to hear the human spirit's OK. How's the
lungs?

(*She takes her stethoscope from her pocket. She puts the stethoscope to* KEN's *chest*)

KEN
(*Sings*)

Boom boom.

DR. SCOTT

Be quiet. You'll deafen me.

KEN

Sorry.
(*She continues to listen*)
And what does it say?

DR. SCOTT
(*Gives up*)

What does what say?

KEN

My heart, of course. What secrets does it tell?

DR. SCOTT

It was just telling me that it's better off than it was six months ago.

KEN

It's a brave heart. It keeps its secrets.

DR. SCOTT

And what are they?

KEN

Did you hear it going boom boom, like that? Two
beats.

DR. SCOTT

Of course.

KEN

Well, I'll tell you. That's because it's broken, broken
in two. But each part carries on bravely, yearning for
a woman in a white coat.

DR. SCOTT

And I thought it was the first and second heart
sounds.

KEN

Ah! Is there a consultant's round this morning?

DR. SCOTT

That's right.

KEN

I suppose he will sweep in here like Zeus from
Olympus, with his attendant nymphs and swains.

DR. SCOTT

I don't think that's fair.

KEN

Why not?

DR. SCOTT

He cares; he cares a lot.

KEN

But what about?

DR. SCOTT

His patients.

KEN

I suppose so.

DR. SCOTT

He does. When you first came in he worked his guts
out to keep you going; he cares.

KEN

I was a bit flip, wasn't I . . .

DR. SCOTT

It's understandable.

KEN

But soon we shall have to ask the question why.

DR. SCOTT

Why?

KEN

Why bother. You remember the mountain labored
and brought forth not a man but a mouse. It was a
big joke. On the mouse. If you're as insignificant as
that, who needs a mountain for a mummy?

DR. SCOTT

I'll see you later . . . with Dr. Emerson.

KEN

And Cupbearers Limited.

DR. SCOTT

Oh no . . . I assure you . . . We're not at all limited.
(*She goes out. She opens the door of* SIS-
TER's *room. The* SISTER *is writing at the
desk*)
Sister. It's Mr. Harrison. He seems a little agitated
this morning.

SISTER

Yes, he's beginning to realize what he's up against.

DR. SCOTT

I'm changing the prescription and putting him on a
small dose of Valium. I'll have a word with Dr.
Emerson. Thank you, Sister.
(*She closes the door and looks up the corridor toward* KEN's *room.* NURSE SADLER *is
just going in with a feeding cup*)

KEN

An acolyte, bearing a cup.

NURSE

I beg your pardon?

KEN

Nothing. I was joking. It's nothing.

NURSE

It's coffee.

KEN

You're joking now.

NURSE

I'm not.

KEN

What you have there is a coffee-flavored milk drink.

NURSE

Don't you like it?

KEN

It's all right, but I would like some real coffee, hot and black and bitter so that I could chew it.

NURSE

I'll ask the Sister.

KEN

I shouldn't.

NURSE

Why not?

KEN

Because in an hour's time, you'll be bringing round a little white pill that is designed to insert rose-colored filters behind my eyes. It will calm me and soothe me and make me forget for a while that you have a lovely body.

NURSE

Mr. Harrison . . . I'm . . .

KEN
(*Genuinely concerned*)
I'm sorry. Really, I *am* sorry. I don't want to take it
out on you—it's not your fault. You're only the vestal
virgin . . . Sorry I said virgin.

NURSE
You'd better drink your coffee before it gets cold.
(*She feeds him a little, sip by sip*)

KEN
I was right; it's milky . . . What made you become a
nurse?

NURSE
I'm not a nurse yet.

KEN
Oh yes you are.
(NURSE SADLER *smiles*)
Nurse Sadler.

NURSE
You must have thought me a real twit.

KEN
Of course not!

NURSE
The Sister-Tutor told us we would say it.

KEN
Well then . . .

NURSE

But I was so sure I wouldn't.

KEN

You haven't told me what made you become a nurse.

NURSE

I've always wanted to. What made you become a sculptor?

KEN

Hey there! You're learning too fast!

NURSE

What do you mean?

KEN

When you get a personal question, just ignore it— change the subject, or better still, ask another question back.

(NURSE SADLER *smiles*)

Did Sister-Tutor tell you that too?

NURSE

Something like it.

KEN

It's called being professional, isn't it?

NURSE

I suppose so.

KEN

I don't want any more of that, it's horrid. Patients are requested not to ask for credit for their intelligence, as refusal often offends.

NURSE

You sound angry. I hope I . . .

KEN

Not with you, Kay. Not at all. With myself I expect. Don't say it. That's futile isn't it?

NURSE

Yes.

     (SISTER *opens the door*)

SISTER

Have you finished, Nurse? Dr. Emerson is here.

NURSE

Yes, Sister. I'm just coming.

SISTER

Straighten that sheet.

     (*She goes, leaving the door open*)

KEN

Hospitals are weird places. Broken necks are acceptable, but a wrinkled sheet! . . .

     (NURSE SADLER *smooths the bed. She goes out as* DR. EMERSON *comes in with* SISTER *and* DR. SCOTT)

DR. EMERSON

Morning.

KEN

Good morning.

DR. EMERSON

How are you this morning?

KEN

As you see, racing around all over the place.
(DR. EMERSON *picks up the chart and notes
from the bottom of the bed*)

DR. EMERSON
(*To* DR. SCOTT)

You've prescribed Valium, I see.

DR. SCOTT

Yes.

DR. EMERSON

His renal function looks much improved.

DR. SCOTT

Yes, the blood urea is back to normal and the cultures are sterile.

DR. EMERSON

Good . . . Good. Well, we had better go on keeping
an eye on it, just in case.

DR. SCOTT

Yes, of course, sir.

DR. EMERSON

Good . . . Well, Mr. Harrison, we seem to be out of
the woods now . . .

KEN

So when are you going to discharge me?

DR. EMERSON

Difficult to say.

KEN

Really? Are you ever going to discharge me?

DR. EMERSON

Well, you'll certainly be leaving *us* soon, I should
think.

KEN

Discharged or transferred?

DR. EMERSON

This unit is for critical patients; when we have
reached a position of stability, then you can be
looked after in a much more comfortable, quiet
hospital.

KEN

You mean you only grow the vegetables here—the
vegetable store is somewhere else.

DR. EMERSON
I don't think I understand you.

KEN
I think you do. Spell it out for me, please. What chance have I of only being partly dependent on nursing?

DR. EMERSON
It's impossible to say with certainty what the prognosis of any case is.

KEN
I'm not asking for a guarantee on oath. I am simply asking for your professional opinion. Do you believe I will ever walk again?

DR. EMERSON
No.

KEN
Or recover the use of my arms?

DR. EMERSON
No.

KEN
Thank you.

DR. EMERSON
What for?

KEN

Your honesty.

DR. EMERSON

Yes, well . . . I should try not to brood on it if I were you. It's surprising how we can come to accept things. Dr. Scott has prescribed something which will help.
(*To* DR. SCOTT)
You might also get Mrs. Boyle along . . .

DR. SCOTT

Yes, of course.

DR. EMERSON

You'll be surprised how many things you will be able to do. Good morning.
(*They go into the corridor area*)

DR. EMERSON

What dose was it you prescribed?

DR. SCOTT

Two milligrams T.I.D.

DR. EMERSON

That's very small. You might have to increase it to five milligrams.

DR. SCOTT

Yes, sir.

DR. EMERSON

We ought to aim to get him moved in a month at
most. These beds are very precious.

DR. SCOTT

Yes.

DR. EMERSON

Well, thank you, Doctor. I must rush off. Damned
committee meeting.

DR. SCOTT

I thought you hated those.

DR. EMERSON

I do, but there's a new heart monitoring unit I want
. . . very much indeed.

DR. SCOTT

Good luck, then.

DR. EMERSON

Thank you, Clare.
        (*He goes.* DR. SCOTT *looks in at* SISTER'*s
                        office.*)

DR. SCOTT

Did you get that Valium for Mr. Harrison, Sister?

SISTER

Yes, Doctor. I was going to give him the first at
twelve o'clock.

DR. SCOTT

Give him one now, will you?

SISTER

Right.

DR. SCOTT

Thank you.
          (*She begins to walk away, then turns*)
On second thoughts . . . give it to me. I'll take it. I
want to talk with him.

SISTER

Here it is.
     (*She hands a small tray with a tablet and a
     feeding cup of water*)

DR. SCOTT

Thank you.
          (*She walks to* KEN's *room and goes in*)
I've brought something to help you.

KEN

My God, they've got some highly qualified nurses
here.

DR. SCOTT

Only the best in this hospital.

KEN

You're spoiling me you know, Doctor. If this goes on
I shall demand that my next enema is performed by
no one less than the Matron.

DR. SCOTT

Well, it wouldn't be the first she'd done, or the thousandth either.

KEN

She worked up through the ranks, did she?

DR. SCOTT

They all do.

KEN

Yes, in training school they probably learn that at the bottom of every bed pan lies a potential Matron. Just now, for one or two glorious minutes, I felt like a human being again.

DR. SCOTT

Good.

KEN

And now you're going to spoil it.

DR. SCOTT

How?

KEN

By tranquilizing yourself.

DR. SCOTT

Me?

KEN

Oh, I shall get the tablet, but it's you that needs the tranquilizing; I don't.

DR. SCOTT

Dr. Emerson and I thought . . .

KEN

You both watched me disturbed, worried even
perhaps, and you can't do anything for me—nothing
that really matters. I'm paralyzed and you're impotent. This disturbs you because you're a sympathe-
tic person and as someone dedicated to an active
sympathy doing something—anything even—you
find it hard to accept you're impotent. The only
thing you can do is to stop me thinking about it—
that is—stop me disturbing you. So I get the tablet
and you get the tranquility.

DR. SCOTT

That's a tough diagnosis.

KEN

Is it so far from the truth?

DR. SCOTT

There may be an element of truth in it, but it's not
the whole story.

KEN

I don't suppose it is.

DR. SCOTT

After all, there is no point in worrying unduly—you
know the facts. It's no use banging your head
against a wall.

KEN

If the only feeling I have is in my head, and I want to feel, I might choose to bang it against a wall.

DR. SCOTT

And if you damage your head?

KEN

You mean go bonkers?

DR. SCOTT

Yes.

KEN

Then that would be the final catastrophe, but I'm not bonkers—yet. My consciousness is the only thing I have and I must claim the right to use it and, as far as possible, act on conclusions I may come to.

DR. SCOTT

Of course.

KEN

Good. Then you eat that tablet if you want tranquility, because I'm not going to.

DR. SCOTT

It is prescribed.

KEN

Oh come off it, Doctor. I know everyone around here acts as though those little bits of paper have

just been handed down from Sinai. But the writing
on those tablets isn't in Hebrew . . .

DR. SCOTT
. . . Well, you aren't due for it till twelve o'clock.
We'll see . . .

KEN
That's what I always say. If you don't know whether
to take a tranquilizer or not—sleep on it. When you
tell Dr. Emerson, impress on him I don't need
it . . .
(DR. SCOTT *smiles. She leaves and goes to
the* SISTER's *room*)

DR. SCOTT
Sister, I haven't given it to him . . . Leave it for a
while.

SISTER
Did you alter the notes?

DR. SCOTT
No . . . Not yet.
(*She picks up a pile of notes and begins
writing*)

(CROSS FADE *on sluice room*)

(NURSE SADLER *is taking kidney dishes and
instruments out of the sterilizer.* JOHN
creeps up behind her and seizes her round

the waist. NURSE SADLER *jumps, utters a*
muffled scream and drops a dish)

NURSE

Oh, it's you . . . Don't do that . . .

JOHN

I couldn't help myself, honest, my Lord. There was
this vision in white and blue, then I saw red in front
of my eyes. It was like looking into a Union Jack.
    (NURSE SADLER *has turned round to face*
    JOHN, *who has his arms either side of her*
    against the table)

NURSE

Let go . . .

JOHN

What's a nice girl like you doing in a place like this?

NURSE

Sterilizing the instruments . . .
        (JOHN *gasps and holds his groin*)

JOHN

Don't say things like that! Just the thought . . .
    (NURSE SADLER *is free and returns to her*
    work)

NURSE

I don't know what you're doing in a place like this
 . . . It's just a big joke to you.

JOHN

'Course it is. You can't take a place like this seriously . . .

NURSE

Why ever not?

JOHN

It's just the ante-room of the morgue.

NURSE

That's terrible! They don't all die.

JOHN

Don't they?

NURSE

No! Old Mr. Trevellyan is going out tomorrow, for instance.

JOHN

After his third heart attack! I hope they give him a return ticket on the ambulance.

NURSE

Would you just let them die? People like Mr. Harrison?

JOHN

How much does it cost to keep him here? Hundreds of pounds a week.

NURSE

That's not the point.

JOHN

In Africa children die of measles. It would cost only
a few pounds to keep them alive. There's something
crazy somewhere.

NURSE

That's wrong too—but it wouldn't help just letting
Mr. Harrison die.

JOHN

No . . .
(He goes up to her again)
Nurse Sadler, when your eyes flash, you send shiv-
ers up and down my spine . . .

NURSE

John, stop it . . .
(She is backing away)

JOHN

Why don't we go out tonight?

NURSE

I've got some work to do for my exam.

JOHN

Let me help . . . I'm an expert on anatomy. We
could go dancing, down to the Barbados Club, a few

drinks and then back to my pad for an anatomy lesson.

NURSE

Let me get on . . .

> (JOHN *holds* NURSE SADLER's *head and slides his hands down*)

JOHN
(*Singing*)

Oh the head bone's connected to the neck bone,
The neck bone's connected to the shoulder bone,
The shoulder bone's connected to the . . . breast
bone . . .

> (NURSE SADLER *escapes just in time. She backs out of the room and into* SISTER, *who is coming to see what's causing the noise.*)

NURSE

Sorry, Sister.

SISTER

This hospital exists to cure accidents, not to cause them.

NURSE

No . . . Yes . . . Sister.

SISTER

Are you going to be all day with that sterilizer?

NURSE

No, Sister.

(*She hurries away*)

SISTER

Haven't you any work to do, John?

JOHN

Sister, my back is bowed down with the weight of all the work resting on it.

SISTER

Then I suggest you shift some.

JOHN

Right.

(*She goes.* JOHN *shrugs and goes*)

(CROSS FADE *on* DR. EMERSON's *office*)

(DR. EMERSON *is on the phone*)

DR. EMERSON

Look, Jenkins, I know the capital cost is high, but it would save on nursing costs. I've got four cardiac cases in here at the moment. With that unit I could save at least on one nurse a day. They could all be monitored in the Sister's room . . . Yes I know . . .

(DR. SCOTT *knocks on the door. She goes in*)

Hello? . . . Yes, well, old chap, I've got to go now. Do impress on the board how much money we'd

save in the long run . . . all right . . . Thank you.
               (*He puts the phone down*)

DR. SCOTT

Still wheeling and dealing for that monitoring unit?

DR. EMERSON

Bloody administrators. In this job a degree in accountancy would be more valuable to me than my M.D. . . . Still, what can I do for you?

DR. SCOTT

It's Harrison.

DR. EMERSON

Some sort of relapse?

DR. SCOTT

On the contrary.

DR. EMERSON

Good.

DR. EMERSON

He doesn't want to take Valium.

DR. EMERSON

Doesn't want to take it? What do you mean?

DR. SCOTT

He guessed it was some sort of tranquilizer and said he preferred to keep his consciousness clear.

DR. EMERSON

That's the trouble with all this anti-drug prop-
aganda; it's useful of course, but it does set up a
negative reaction to even necessary drugs, in sensitive people.

DR. SCOTT

I'm not sure he's not right.

DR. EMERSON

Right? When you prescribed the drug, you thought
he needed it.

DR. SCOTT

Yes.

DR. EMERSON

And when I saw him, I agreed with you.

DR. SCOTT

Yes.

DR. EMERSON

It's a very small dose—two milligrams T.I.D. wasn't
it?

DR. SCOTT

That's right.

DR. EMERSON

The minimum that will have any effect at all. You
remember I said you might have to go up to five

milligrams. A psychiatric dose, you know, is ten or
fifteen miligrams.

DR. SCOTT

I know, but Mr. Harrison isn't a psychiatric case, is
he?

DR. EMERSON

So how did you persuade him to take it?

DR. SCOTT

I didn't.

DR. EMERSON

Now let's get this clear. This morning when you
examined him, you came to a careful and responsible decision that your patient needed a certain drug.

DR. SCOTT

Yes.

DR. EMERSON

I saw the patient and I agreed with your prescription.

DR. SCOTT

Yes.

DR. EMERSON

But in spite of two qualified opinions, you accept
the decision of someone completely unqualified to
take it.

DR. SCOTT

He may be unqualified, but he is the one affected.

DR. EMERSON

Ours was an objective, his a subjective decision.

DR. SCOTT

But isn't this a case where a subjective decision may be more valid? After all, you're both working on the same subject—his body. Only he knows more about how he feels.

DR. EMERSON

But he doesn't know about the drugs and their effects.

DR. SCOTT

He can feel their effects directly.

DR. EMERSON

Makes no difference. His knowledge isn't based on experience of a hundred such cases. He can't know enough to challenge our clinical decisions.

DR. SCOTT

That's what he's doing and he's protesting about the dulling of his consciousness with Valium.

DR. EMERSON

When he came in, shocked to hell, did he protest about the dextrose-saline? Or when he was gasping for breath, he didn't use some of it to protest about the aminophylline or the huge stat dose of cortisone . . .

DR. SCOTT
Those were inevitable and emergency decisions.

DR. EMERSON
And so is this one inevitable. Just because our patient is conscious, that does not absolve us from our complete responsibility. We have to maximize whatever powers he retains.

DR. SCOTT
And how does a depressant drug improve his consciousness?

DR. EMERSON
It will help him to use his consciousness, Clare. We must help him now to turn his mind to the real problem he has. We must help him to an acceptance of his condition. Only then will his full consciousness be any use to him at all . . . You say he refused to take the tablet?

> (DR. SCOTT *nods*. DR. EMERSON *picks up the phone and dials. The phone rings in the* SISTER's *office*)

SISTER
Sister Anderson speaking.

DR. EMERSON
Emerson here. Could you prepare a syringe with five milligrams of Valium for Mr. Harrison?

SISTER
Yes, sir.

DR. EMERSON
I'll be down myself immediately to give it to him.

SISTER
Yes, sir.
> (*She replaces the phone and immediately prepares the syringe*)

DR. SCOTT
Do you want me to come?

DR. EMERSON
No . . . It won't be necessary.

DR. SCOTT
Thank you . . . .
> (*She moves to the door*)

DR. EMERSON
Harrison is an intelligent, sensitive and articulate man.

DR. SCOTT
Yes.

DR. EMERSON
But don't undervalue yourself. Clare, your first decision was right.
> (DR. SCOTT *nods and leaves the room. She is unhappy.* DR. EMERSON *walks to the* SISTER'*s room*)

DR. EMERSON

Have you the Valium ready, Sister?

SISTER

Yes, sir.
 (*She hands him the kidney dish.* DR. EMER-
 SON *takes it.* SISTER *makes to follow him*)

DR. EMERSON

It's all right, Sister. You've plenty of work, I expect.

SISTER

There's always plenty of that.
 (DR. EMERSON *goes into* KEN's *room*)

KEN

Hello, hello, they've brought up the heavy brigade.
 (DR. EMERSON *pulls back the bed clothes
 and reaches for* KEN's *arm*)
Dr. Emerson, I am afraid I must insist that you do
not stick that needle in me.

DR. EMERSON

It is important that I do.

KEN

Who for?

DR. EMERSON

You.

KEN

I'm the best judge of that.

DR. EMERSON

I think not. You don't even know what's in this syringe.

KEN

I take it that the injection is one of a series of measures to keep me alive.

DR. EMERSON

You could say that.

KEN

Then it is not important. I've decided not to stay alive.

DR. EMERSON

But you can't decide that.

KEN

Why not?

DR. EMERSON

You're very depressed.

KEN

Does that surprise you?

DR. EMERSON

Of course not; it's perfectly natural. Your body received massive injuries; it takes time to come to any acceptance of the new situation. Now I shan't be a minute . . .

KEN

Don't stick that fucking thing in me!

DR. EMERSON

There . . . It's over now.

KEN

Doctor, I didn't give you permission to stick that
needle in me. Why did you do it?

DR. EMERSON

It was necessary. Now try to sleep . . . You will find
that as you gain acceptance of the situation you will
be able to find a new way of living.

KEN

Please let me make myself clear. I specifically refused permission to stick that needle in me and you
didn't listen. You took no notice.

DR. EMERSON

You must rely on us, old chap. Of course you're depressed. I'll send someone along to have a chat with
you. Now I really must go and get on with my
rounds.

KEN

Doctor . . .

DR. EMERSON

I'll send someone along.
        (*He places the dish on the side locker,
        throwing the needle in a waste bin. He*

(*goes out.* KEN *is frustrated and then his eyes close*)

(*CROSS FADE on* SISTER's *office*)

(SISTER *and* DR. SCOTT *are sitting*)

SISTER
I'm always warning my nurses not to get involved.

DR. SCOTT
Of course . . . And you never do, do you?

SISTER
(*Smiling*)
. . . Never.

DR. SCOTT
You're a liar, Sister.

SISTER
Dr. Scott!

DR. SCOTT
Come on, we all do. Dr. Emerson is as involved with Ken Harrison as if he were his father.

SISTER
But you don't feel like his mother!

DR. SCOTT
. . . No comment, Sister.
(NURSE SADLER *comes into* SISTER's *office*)

NURSE

I've finished, Sister.

SISTER

All right . . . Off you go then, Nurse.

NURSE

Yes, Sister!

SISTER

Have you been running?

NURSE

No, Sister!

SISTER

Oh . . . You just looked . . . flushed.

NURSE

. . . Oh . . . Goodnight, Sister . . . Doctor.

SISTER }
DR. SCOTT}

Goodnight.

(CROSS FADE *to* KEN's *room*)

(SISTER *and* NURSE SADLER *come in with
the trolley*)

SISTER

Good morning, Mr. Harrison. How are you this
morning?

KEN

Marvelous.

SISTER

Night Sister said you slept well.

KEN

I did. I had a lot of help, remember.

SISTER

Your eyes are bright this morning.

KEN

I've been thinking.

SISTER

You do too much of that.

KEN

What other activity would you suggest? . . . Football? I tell you what, Sister, just leave me alone with Nurse Sadler here. Let's see what the old Adam can do for me.

SISTER

I'm a Sister, not a Madame.

KEN

Sister—you dark horse you! All this time you've been kidding me. I've been wondering for months how on earth a woman could become a State Registered Nurse and a Sister and still think you found babies under a gooseberry bush—and you've known all along.

SISTER

Of course I've known. When I qualified as a midwife I learnt that when they pick up the babies from under the gooseberry bushes they wrap them up in women to keep them warm. I know because it was our job to unwrap them again.

KEN

The miracle of modern science! Anyway, Sister, as I said, I've been thinking, if I'm going to be around for a long time, money will help.

SISTER

It always does.

KEN

Do you remember that solicitor chap representing my insurance company a few months ago? Mr. Hill, I think he said his name was. He said he'd come back when I felt better. Do you think you could get him back as soon as possible? I'd feel more settled if we could get the compensation sorted out.

SISTER

Sounds a good idea.

KEN

You'll ring him up?

SISTER

Of course.

KEN

He left a card; it's in my drawer.

SISTER

Right.
(She goes to the locker and takes out the card)
Mr. Philip Hill, Solicitor. Right, I'll ring him.

KEN

Thanks.

SISTER

That's enough.
(They cover him up again and straighten the bed)

SISTER

Mrs. Boyle is waiting to see you, Mr. Harrison.

KEN

Mrs. Boyle? Who's she?

SISTER

A very nice woman.

KEN

Oh God, must I see her?

SISTER

Dr. Emerson asked her to come along.

KEN

Then I'd better see her. If I refuse, he'll probably
dissolve her in water and inject her into me.
(SISTER *has to choke back a giggle*)

SISTER

Mr. Harrison! Come on, Nurse; this man will be the
death of me.

KEN
(*Cheerfully*)

Doubt it, Sister. I'm not even able to be the death of
myself.
(SISTER *goes out with* NURSE SADLER. MRS.
GILLIAN BOYLE *enters. She is thirty-five,
attractive, and very professional in her
manner. She is a medical social worker*)

MRS. BOYLE

Good morning.

KEN

Morning.

MRS. BOYLE

Mr. Harrison?

KEN
(*Cheerfully*)

It used to be.

MRS. BOYLE

My name is Mrs. Boyle.

KEN

And you've come to cheer me up.

MRS. BOYLE

I wouldn't put it like that.

KEN

How would you put it?

MRS. BOYLE

I've come to see if I can help.

KEN

Good. You can.

MRS. BOYLE

How?

KEN

Go and convince Dr. Frankenstein that he has suc-
cessfully made his monster and he can now let it go.

MRS. BOYLE

Dr. Emerson is a first-rate physician. My goodness,
they have improved this room.

KEN

Have they?

MRS. BOYLE

It used to be really dismal. All dark green and

cream. It's surprising what pastel colors will do,
isn't it? Really cheerful.

KEN

Yes; perhaps they should try painting me. I'd hate to
be the thing that ruins the decor.

MRS. BOYLE

What on earth makes you say that? You don't ruin
anything.

KEN

I'm sorry. That was a bit . . . whining. Well, don't
let me stop you.

MRS. BOYLE

Doing what?

KEN

What you came for, I suppose. What do you do?
Conjuring tricks? Funny stories? Or a belly dance?
If I have any choice, I'd prefer the belly dance.

MRS. BOYLE

I'm afraid I've left my bikini at home.

KEN

Who said anything about a bikini?

MRS. BOYLE

Dr. Emerson tells me that you don't want any more
treatment.

KEN

Good.

MRS. BOYLE

Why good?

KEN

I didn't think he'd heard what I'd said.

MRS. BOYLE

Why not?

KEN

He didn't take any notice.

MRS. BOYLE

Well as you can see, he did.

KEN

He sent you?

MRS. BOYLE

Yes.

KEN

And you are my new treatment; get in.

MRS. BOYLE

Why don't you want any more treatment?

KEN

I'd rather not go on living like this.

MRS. BOYLE

Why not?

KEN

Isn't it obvious?

MRS. BOYLE

Not to me. I've seen many patients like you.

KEN

And they all want to live?

MRS. BOYLE

Usually.

KEN

Why?

MRS. BOYLE

They find a new way of life.

KEN

How?

MRS. BOYLE

You'll be surprised how many things you will be able to do with training and a little patience.

KEN

Such as?

MRS. BOYLE

We can't be sure yet. But I should think that you will be able to operate reading machines and perhaps an adapted typewriter.

KEN

Reading and writing. What about arithmetic?

MRS. BOYLE
(*Smiling*)

I dare say we could fit you up with a comptometer if you really wanted one.

KEN

Mrs. Boyle, even educationalists have realized that the three r's do not make a full life.

MRS. BOYLE

What did you do before the accident?

KEN

I taught in an art school. I was a sculptor.

MRS. BOYLE

I see.

KEN

Difficult, isn't it? How about an electrically operated hammer and chisel? No, well. Or a cybernetic lump of clay?

MRS. BOYLE

I wouldn't laugh if I were you. It's amazing what can be done. Our scientists are wonderful.

KEN

They are. But it's not good enough you see, Mrs. Boyle. I really have absolutely no desire at all to be the object of scientific virtuosity. I have thought things over very carefully. I do have plenty of time for thinking and I have decided that I do not want to go on living with so much effort for so little result.

MRS. BOYLE

Yes, well, we shall have to see about that.

KEN

What is there to see?

MRS. BOYLE

We can't just stop treatment, just like that.

KEN

Why not?

MRS. BOYLE

It's the job of the hospital to save life, not to lose it.

KEN

The hospital's done all it can, but it wasn't enough. It wasn't the hospital's fault; the original injury was too big.

MRS. BOYLE

We have to make the best of the situation.

KEN

No. "We" don't have to do anything. I have to do what is to be done and that is to cash in the chips.

MRS. BOYLE

It's not unusual, you know, for people injured as you have been, to suffer with this depression for a

considerable time before they begin to see that a
life is possible.

KEN

How long?

MRS. BOYLE

It varies.

KEN

Don't hedge.

MRS. BOYLE

It could be a year or so.

KEN

And it could last for the rest of my life.

MRS. BOYLE

That would be most unlikely.

KEN

I'm sorry, but I cannot settle for that.

MRS. BOYLE

Try not to dwell on it. I'll see what I can do to get
you started on some occupational therapy. Perhaps
we could make a start on the reading machines.

KEN

Do you have many books for those machines?

MRS. BOYLE

Quite a few.

KEN

Can I make a request for the first one?

MRS. BOYLE

If you like.

KEN

"How to be a sculptor with no hands."

MRS. BOYLE

I'll be back tomorrow with the machine.

KEN

It's marvelous, you know.

MRS. BOYLE

What is?

KEN

All you people have the same technique. When I say something really awkward you just pretend I haven't said anything at all. You're all the bloody same . . . Well there's another outburst. That should be your cue to comment on the light-shade or the color of the walls.

MRS. BOYLE

I'm sorry if I have upset you.

KEN

Of course you have upset me. You and the doctors with your appalling so-called professionalism,

which is nothing more than a series of verbal tricks
to prevent you relating to your patients as human
beings.

MRS. BOYLE
You must understand; we have to remain relatively
detached in order to help . . .

KEN
That's all right with me. Detach yourself. Tear yourself off on the dotted line that divides the woman
from the social worker and post yourself off to
another patient.

MRS. BOYLE
You're very upset . . . .

KEN
Christ Almighty, you're doing it again. Listen to
yourself, woman. I say something offensive about
you and you turn your professional cheek. If you
were human, if you were treating me as human,
you'd tell me to bugger off. Can't you see that this is
why I've decided that life isn't worth living? I am
not human and I'm even more convinced of that by
your visit than I was before, so how does that grab
you? The very exercise of your so-called professionalism makes me want to die.

MRS. BOYLE
I'm . . . Please . . .

KEN

Go . . . For God's sake get out . . . Go on . . . Get
out . . . Get out.
    (*She goes into* SISTER'*s room.* SISTER *hears*
    KEN'*s shouts*)

SISTER

What's the matter, Mrs. Boyle?

MRS. BOYLE

It's Mr. Harrison . . . He seems very upset.

KEN
(*Shouting*)
. . . I am upset.
            (SISTER *closes the door*)

SISTER

I should leave him for now, Mrs. Boyle. We'll send
for you again when he's better.
    (SISTER *hurries in to* KEN. *He is very dis-*
    tressed, rocking his head from side to side,
    desperately short of breath)

KEN

Sis . . . ter . . .
            (SISTER *reaches for the oxygen mask*)

SISTER

Now, now, Mr. Harrison, calm down.
    (*She applies the mask and turns on the*
    oxygen. KEN *gradually becomes calmer*)

Tony Mazze

SISTER

Now why do you go getting yourself so upset? . . .
There's no point . . .

KEN
(*Muffled*)

But . . .

SISTER

Stop talking, Mr. Harrison. Just relax.
>   (KEN *becomes calm.* SISTER *sees* NURSE
>   SADLER *going past.* MRS. BOYLE *is still
>   hovering*)

Nurse.

NURSE

Sister?

SISTER

Take over here, will you?

NURSE

Yes, Sister.
>   (NURSE SADLER *holds the mask.* SISTER
>   *goes to the door*)

MRS. BOYLE

Is he all right?

SISTER

Yes, perfectly.

MRS. BOYLE
I'm sorry . . .

SISTER
Don't worry. It was not you . . . We'll let you know when he's better.

MRS. BOYLE
Right . . . Thank you.
>(*She goes.* SISTER *stands at the open door*)

SISTER
Just give him another ten seconds, Nurse.

NURSE
Yes, Sister.
>(SISTER *takes a pace back behind the door and listens. After ten seconds,* NURSE SAD-LER *removes the mask*)

KEN
Oh, she's a shrewd cookie, is our Sister.
>(SISTER *smiles at this.* NURSE SADLER *glances backward.* KEN *catches on to the reason*)

It's all right, Sister. I'm still alive, bugger it. I don't want to give her too much satisfaction.

NURSE
She's gone.
>(*She closes the door*)

KEN

Come on then, over here. I shan't bite you, Kay.
Come and cool my fevered brow or something.

NURSE

What upset you?

KEN

Being patronized, I suppose.

NURSE

What did you mean about Sister?

KEN

She knew if she came in I'd shout at her, but if you
were here I wouldn't shout.

NURSE

Why?

KEN

A good question. Because I suppose you're young
and gentle and innocent and Sister knows that I am
not the sort who would shout at you . . .

NURSE

You mean, you would rather patronize me.

KEN

Hey! Steady on there, Kay. If you show you're well
able to take care of yourself I shall have to call you

Nurse Sadler and shout at you too, and Sister and I
will have lost a valuable asset.

NURSE

What were you? . . .
> (*The door opens and* SISTER *and* DR. SCOTT
> *come in*)

KEN

What is this? Piccadilly Circus?

SISTER

All right, Nurse. Dr. Scott was just coming as it happened. Are you feeling better now, Mr. Harrison?
> (NURSE SADLER *leaves*)

KEN

Lovely, thank you, Sister.

SISTER

I made your phone call to Mr. Hill. He said he'd try
to get in tomorrow.

KEN

Thank you . . .
> (SISTER *leaves*)

DR. SCOTT

And what was all the fuss about?

KEN

I'm sorry about that. The last thing I want is to bring
down Emerson again with his pharmaceutical
truncheon.

DR. SCOTT

I'm . . . sorry about that.

KEN

I don't suppose it was your fault.

DR. SCOTT

Can I give you some advice?

KEN

Please do; I may even take it.

DR. SCOTT

Take the tablets; the dose is very small—the minimum—and it won't really blunt your consciousness, not like the injection.

KEN

. . . You're on.

DR. SCOTT

Good . . . I was glad to hear about your decision to try and get your compensation settled.

KEN

How did you? . . . Oh, I suppose Sister checked with you.

DR. SCOTT

She did mention it . . .

KEN

You have lovely breasts.

DR. SCOTT

I beg your pardon?

KEN

I said you have lovely breasts.

DR. SCOTT

What an odd thing to say.

KEN

Why? You're not only a doctor, are you? You can't
tell me that you regard them only as mammary
glands.

DR. SCOTT

No.

KEN

You're quite safe.

DR. SCOTT

Of course.

KEN

I'm not about to jump out of bed and rape you or
anything.

DR. SCOTT

I know.

KEN

Did it embarrass you?

DR. SCOTT

Surprised me.

KEN

And embarrassed you.

DR. SCOTT

I suppose so.

KEN

But why exactly? You are an attractive woman. I
admit that it's unusual for a man to compliment a
woman on her breasts when only one of them is in
bed, only one of the people that is, not one of the
breasts, but that wasn't the reason, was it?

DR. SCOTT

I don't think it helps you to talk like this.

KEN

Because I can't do anything about it, you mean.

DR. SCOTT

I didn't mean that exactly.

KEN

I watch you walking in the room, bending over me,
tucking in your sweater. It's surprising how relaxed
a woman can become when she is not in the presence of a man.

DR. SCOTT

I am sorry if I provoked you . . . I can assure
you . . .

KEN

You haven't "provoked" me, as you put it, but you
are a woman and even though I've only a piece of
knotted string between my legs, I still have a man's
mind. One change that I have noticed is that I now
engage in sexual banter with your nurses, searching
for the double entendre in the most innocent re-
mark. Like a sexually desperate middle-aged man.
Then they leave the room and I go cold with embar-
rassment. It's fascinating, isn't it? Laughable. I still
have tremendous sexual desire. Do you find that
disgusting?

DR. SCOTT

No.

KEN

Pathetic?

DR. SCOTT

Sad.

KEN

I am serious you know . . . about deciding to die.

DR. SCOTT

You will get over that feeling.

KEN

How do you know?

DR. SCOTT

From experience.

KEN

That doesn't alter the validity of my decision now.

DR. SCOTT

But if we acted on your decision now, there wouldn't be an opportunity for you to accept it.

KEN

I grant you, I may become lethargic and quiescent. Happy when a nurse comes to put in a new catheter, or give me an enema, or to turn me over. These could become the high spots of my day. I might even learn to do wonderful things, like turn the pages of a book with some miracle of modern science, or to type letters with flicking my eyelids. And you would look at me and say: "Wasn't it worth waiting?" and I would say: "Yes" and be proud of my achievements. Really proud. I grant you all that, but it doesn't alter the validity of my present position.

DR. SCOTT

But if you became happy?

KEN

But I don't want to become happy by becoming the computer section of a complex machine. And morally, you must accept my decision.

DR. SCOTT

Not according to my morals.

KEN

And why are yours better than mine? They're better because you're more powerful. I am in your power. To hell with a morality that is based on the proposition that might is right.

DR. SCOTT

I must go now. I was halfway through Mr. Patel.
(*She walks to the door*)

KEN

I thought you were just passing. Oh, Doctor . . . one more thing . . .

DR. SCOTT

Yes?

KEN

You still have lovely breasts.
(*She smiles and goes out into the* SISTER's *office. She is very upset.* SISTER *passes and looks at her*)

SISTER

Are you all right? Would you like a cup of tea?

DR. SCOTT

Yes, Sister, I would.

SISTER

. . . Nurse! Would you bring a cup of tea, please.
(NURSE SADLER *looks from the kitchen*)

NURSE

Yes, Sister.

(They walk into the SISTER's *room and sit down)*

DR. SCOTT

I've never met anyone like Ken Harrison before.

SISTER

No.

DR. SCOTT

He's so . . . bright . . . intelligent . . . . He says he wants to die.

SISTER

Many patients say that.

DR. SCOTT

I know that, Sister, but he means it. It's just a calm rational decision.

SISTER

I thought this morning, when he was talking about the compensation, he was beginning to plan for the future.

DR. SCOTT

Not really, you know. That was just to keep us happy. He probably thinks that if he pretends to be planning for the future we'll stop tranquilizing him, or something like that.

(A knock on the door)

SISTER

Come in.

NURSE

Here's the tea, Sister.

SISTER

Thank you, Nurse. For Doctor.
(NURSE SADLER *gives the cup to* DR. SCOTT
and goes out)

DR. SCOTT

It's marvelous, you know. We bring him back to life using everything we've got. We give him back his consciousness, then he says: "But how do I use it?" So what do we do? We put him back to sleep.

(CROSS FADE *on* KEN's *room*)

JOHN *goes in to empty the rubbish. He taps*
KEN *lightly as if to repeat the steel band*
game, but KEN *is asleep*)

JOHN

Ping-Pong . . . You poor bastard.
(*He leaves*)

CURTAIN

ACT TWO

SISTER
A visitor for you, Mr. Harrison.

HILL
Good afternoon, Mr. Harrison.

KEN
Good afternoon.

HILL
You're looking very much better.
(SISTER *has placed a chair by the bed*)

KEN
It's the nursing, you know.

SISTER
I'm glad you realize it, Mr. Harrison.

KEN
Oh I do, Sister, I do.

SISTER

I'll leave you gentlemen now.

HILL

Thank you, Sister.
> (*She goes out*)

You really do look better.

KEN

Yes. I'm as well now as I shall ever be . . .

HILL
> (*Unzipping his briefcase*)

I've brought all the papers . . . Things are moving
along very satisfactorily now and . . .

KEN

I don't want to talk about the accident.

HILL

I understand it must be very distressing . . .

KEN

No, no. It's not that. I didn't get you along about the
compensation.

HILL

Oh . . . Sister said on the phone . . .

KEN

Yes, I know. Could you come away from the door?
Look, do you work for yourself? I mean, you don't

work for an insurance company or something, do
you? . . .

HILL
No. I'm in practice as a solicitor, but I . . .

KEN
Then there's no reason why you couldn't represent
me generally . . . apart from this compensation
thing . . .

HILL
Certainly, if there's anything I can do . . .

KEN
There is.

HILL
Yes?

KEN
. . . Get me out of here.

HILL
. . . I don't understand, Mr. Harrison.

KEN
It's quite simple. I can't exist outside the hospital,
so they've got to keep me here if they want to keep
me alive and they seem intent on doing that. I've
decided that I don't want to stay in hospital any
longer.

HILL

But surely they wouldn't keep you here longer than necessary?

KEN

I'm almost completely paralyzed and I always will be. I shall never be discharged by the hospital. I have coolly and calmly thought it out and I have decided that I would rather not go on. I therefore want to be discharged to die.

HILL

And you want me to represent you?

KEN

Yes. Tough.

HILL

. . . And what is the hospital's attitude?

KEN

They don't know about it yet. Even tougher.

HILL

This is an enormous step . . .

KEN

Mr. Hill, with all respect, I know that our hospitals are wonderful. I know that many people have succeeded in making good lives with appalling handicaps. I'm happy for them and respect and admire them. But each man must make his own decision.

And mine is to die quietly and with as much dignity as I can muster and I need your help.

HILL

Do you realize what you're asking me to do?

KEN

I realize. I'm not asking that you make any decision about my life and death, merely that you represent me and my views to the hospital.

HILL

. . . Yes, well, the first thing is to see the Doctor. What is his name?

KEN

Dr. Emerson.

HILL

I'll try and see him now and come back to you.

KEN

Then you'll represent me? . . .

HILL

Mr. Harrison, I'll let you know my decision after I've seen Dr. Emerson.

KEN

All right, but you'll come back to tell me yourself, even if he convinces you he's right?

HILL

Yes, I'll come back.

(CROSS FADE on the sluice room)

(NURSE SADLER and JOHN are talking)

JOHN

So why not? . . .

NURSE

It's just that I'm so busy . . .

JOHN

All work and no play . . . makes for a boring day.

NURSE

Anyway, I hardly know you.

JOHN

Right . . . That's why I want to take you out . . . to
find out what goes on behind those blue eyes . . .

NURSE

At present, there's just lists of bones and organs, all
getting themselves jumbled up.

JOHN

Because you're working too hard . . .

NURSE

Ask me next week . . .

JOHN
OK. It's a deal . . .

NURSE
Right!

JOHN
And I'll ask you this afternoon as well.

(*CROSS FADE on* DR. EMERSON's *room*)

DR. EMERSON
Mr. Hill? Sister just rang through.

HILL
Dr. Emerson?
                    (*They shake hands*)

DR. EMERSON
You've been seeing Mr. Harrison?

HILL
Yes.

DR. EMERSON
Tragic case . . . I hope you'll be able to get enough
money for him to ease his mind.

HILL
Dr. Emerson. It's not about that I wanted to see you.
I thought I was coming about that, but Mr. Harrison
wishes to retain me to represent him on quite
another matter.

DR. EMERSON

Oh?

HILL

Yes, he wants to be discharged.

DR. EMERSON

That's impossible.

HILL

Why?

DR. EMERSON

To put it bluntly, he would die if we did that.

HILL

He knows that. It's what he wants.

DR. EMERSON

And you are asking me to kill my patient?

HILL

I am representing Mr. Harrison's wishes to you and asking for your reaction.

DR. EMERSON

Well, you've had it. It's impossible. Now if that's really all you came about . . .

HILL

Dr. Emerson, you can, of course, dismiss me like that if you choose to, but I would hardly think it serves anyone's interests, least of all Mr. Harrison's.

DR. EMERSON
I am trying to save Mr. Harrison's life. There is no
need to remind me of my duty to my patient, Mr.
Hill.

HILL
Or mine to my client, Dr. Emerson.

DR. EMERSON
. . . Are you telling me that you have accepted the
job of coming to me to urge a course of action that
will lose your client his life?

HILL
I hadn't accepted it . . . no . . . I told Mr. Harrison
I would talk to you first. Now I have and I begin to
see why he thought it necessary to be represented.

DR. EMERSON
All right . . . Let's start again. Now tell me what
you want to know.

HILL
Mr. Harrison wishes to be discharged from hospital.
Will you please make the necessary arrangements?

DR. EMERSON
No.

HILL
May I ask why not?

DR. EMERSON

Because Mr. Harrison is incapable of living outside the hospital and it is my duty as a doctor to preserve life.

HILL

I take it that Mr. Harrison is a voluntary patient here.

DR. EMERSON

Of course.

HILL

Then I fail to see the legal basis for your refusal.

DR. EMERSON

Can't you understand that Mr. Harrison is suffering from depression? He is incapable of making a rational decision about his life and death.

HILL

Are you maintaining that Mr. Harrison is mentally unbalanced?

DR. EMERSON

Yes.

HILL

Would you have any objection to my bringing in a psychiatrist for a second opinion?

DR. EMERSON

Of course not, but why not ask the consultant

psychiatrist here? I'm sure he will be able to convince you.

HILL
Has he examined Mr. Harrison?

DR. EMERSON
No, but that can be quickly arranged.

HILL
That's very kind of you Dr. Emerson, but I'm sure you'll understand if I ask for my own—whose opinion you are not sure of *before* he examines the patient.

DR. EMERSON
Good afternoon, Mr. Hill.

HILL
Good afternoon.
(MR. HILL *takes up his briefcase and leaves*)

DR.EMERSON
(*Picks up the phone*)
Could you find out where Dr. Travers is, please? I want to see him urgently, and put me through to the hospital secretary, please. Well, put me through when he's free.

(*CROSS FADE on* KEN's *room*)

(*The door opens and* MR. HILL *comes in*)

KEN

Well, how was it on Olympus?

HILL

Cloudy.

KEN

No joy then?

HILL

Dr. Emerson does not wish to discharge you.

KEN

Surprise, surprise. So what do we do now?

HILL

Mr. Harrison, I will be perfectly plain. Dr. Emerson claims that you are not in a sufficiently healthy mental state to make a rational decision, especially one of this seriousness and finality. Now, my position is, I am not competent to decide whether or not he is right.

KEN

So how will you decide?

HILL

I should like to have you examined by an independent psychiatrist and I will accept his view of the case and advise you accordingly.

KEN

Fair enough. Will Dr. Emerson agree?

HILL

He has already. I ought to warn you that Dr. Emerson is likely to take steps to have you admitted here as a person needing treatment under the Mental Health Act of 1959. This means that he can keep you here and give you what treatment he thinks fit.

KEN

Can he do that?

HILL

He probably can.

KEN

Haven't I any say in this?

HILL

Oh yes. He will need another signature and that doctor will have to be convinced that you ought compulsorily to be detained. Even if he agrees, we can appeal.

KEN

Let's get on with it then.

HILL

One thing at a time. First, you remember, our own psychiatrist.

KEN

Wheel him in . . .

HILL

I'll be in touch soon then.

KEN

Oh, before you go. Yesterday I refused to take a tranquilizer and Dr. Emerson came and gave me an injection. It made me pretty dopey. If I was like that when the psychiatrist came, he'd lock me up for life!

HILL

I'll mention it to him. Goodbye for now then.

KEN

Goodbye.

Ken has won 1st

(*CROSS FADE on* DR. EMERSON's *office*)

Battle

(DR. EMERSON *is on the phone*. DR. TRAVERS *knocks on his door and looks in*)

DR. EMERSON

Can you find me Dr. Scott please?
(*He puts the phone down*)

DR. TRAVERS

You wanted to see me?

DR. EMERSON

Ah yes. If you can spare a moment.

DR. TRAVERS

What's the problem?

DR. EMERSON

Nasty one really. I have a road accident case, paralyzed from the neck down. He's naturally very depressed and wants to discharge himself. But with a neurogenic bladder and all the rest of it, he couldn't last a week out of here. I need time to get him used to the idea.

DR. TRAVERS
How long ago was the accident?

DR. EMERSON
Six months.

DR. TRAVERS
A long time.

DR. EMERSON
Yes, well there were other injuries but we've just about got him physically stabilized. The trouble is that he's got himself a solicitor and if I am to keep him here, I'll have to admit him compulsorily under the Mental Health Act. I wondered if you'd see him.

DR. TRAVERS
I'll see him of course, but my signature won't help you.

DR. EMERSON
Why not? You're the psychiatrist, aren't you?

DR. TRAVERS
Yes, but under the Act, you need two signatures and only one can come from a practitioner of the hospital where the patient is to be kept.

DR. EMERSON
Bloody hell!

DR. TRAVERS

Not to worry. I take it you regard this as an emergency.

DR. EMERSON

Of course I do.

DR. TRAVERS

Well, sign the application and then you've got three days to get another signature.

DR. EMERSON

There'll be no problem about that surely?

DR. TRAVERS

Depends upon whether he's clinically depressed or not.

DR. EMERSON

You haven't understood. He's suicidal. He's determined to kill himself.

DR. TRAVERS

I could name you several psychiatrists who wouldn't take that as evidence of insanity.

DR. EMERSON

Well, I could name several psychiatrists who *are* evidence of insanity. I've had a lot of experience in this kind of case. I'm sure, absolutely sure, I can win him around, given time—a few months . . .

DR. TRAVERS

I understand, Michael.

DR. EMERSON

. . . So you'll look at him, will you? . . . And get another chap in? . . .

DR. TRAVERS

Yes, I'll do that.

DR. EMERSON
(*Twinkling*)

And . . . do me a favor, will you? Try and find an old codger like me, who believes in something better than suicide.

DR. TRAVERS
(*Grinning*)

There's a chap at Ellertree . . . a very staunch Catholic, I believe. Would that suit you?

DR. EMERSON

Be Jasus—sounds just the man!

DR. TRAVERS

I'll see his notes and drop in on him . . .

DR. EMERSON

Thank you very much, Paul . . . I'm very grateful—and Harrison will be too.
          (DR. SCOTT *comes in the room*)

DR. SCOTT

Oh, sorry.

DR. TRAVERS

It's all right . . . I'm just off . . . I'll see him then, Michael, this afternoon.

(DR. TRAVERS *leaves*. DR. SCOTT *looks at*
DR. EMERSON *questioningly*)

DR. SCOTT

You wanted me?

DR. EMERSON

Ah yes. Harrison's decided to discharge himself.

DR. SCOTT

Oh no, but I'm not surprised.

DR. EMERSON

So, Travers is seeing him now.

DR. SCOTT

Dr. Travers won't make him change his mind.

DR. EMERSON

I am committing him under Section 26.

DR. SCOTT

Oh, will Dr. Travers sign it?

DR. EMERSON

Evidently if I do, he can't, but he knows a chap over
in Ellertree who probably will.

DR. SCOTT

I see.

DR. EMERSON

I have no choice, do you see, Clare? He's got himself a solicitor. It's the only way I can keep him
here.

DR. SCOTT

Are you sure you should?

DR. EMERSON

Of course. No question.

DR. SCOTT

It's his life.

DR. EMERSON

But my responsibility.

DR. SCOTT

Only if he's incapable of making his own decision.

DR. EMERSON

But he isn't capable. I refuse to believe that a man with a mind as quick as his, a man with enormous mental resources, would calmly choose suicide.

DR. SCOTT

But he has done just that.

DR. EMERSON

And, therefore, I say he is unbalanced.

DR. SCOTT

But surely a wish to die is not *necessarily* a symptom of insanity? A man might want to die for perfectly sane reasons.

DR. EMERSON

No, Clare, a doctor cannot accept the choice for death; he's committed to life. When a patient is

brought into my unit, he's in a bad way. I don't
stand about thinking whether or not it's worth saving his life, I haven't the time for doubts. I get in
there, do whatever I can to save life. I'm a doctor,
not a judge.

DR. SCOTT

I hope you will forgive me sir, for saying this, but I
think that is just how you are behaving—as a judge.

DR. EMERSON

You must, of course, say what you think—but I am
the responsible person here.

DR. SCOTT

I know that sir.
> (*She makes to go*)

DR. EMERSON

I'm sure it's not necessary for me to say this but I'd
rather there was no question of misunderstanding
later . . . Mr. Harrison is now physically stable.
There is no reason why he should die; if he should
die suddenly, I would think it necessary to order a
post-mortem and to act on whatever was found.

DR. SCOTT

. . . Mr. Harrison is your patient, sir.

DR. EMERSON
(*Smiling*)

Of course, of course. You make that sound a fate
worse than death.

DR. SCOTT

Perhaps for him it is.

(*She goes out*)

(*CROSS FADE on* KEN's *room*)
(DR. TRAVERS *comes in*)

DR. TRAVERS

Mr. Harrison?

KEN

That's right.

DR. TRAVERS

Dr. Travers.

KEN

Are you a psychiatrist?

DR. TRAVERS

Yes.

KEN

For or against me . . . Or does that sound like
paranoia?

DR. TRAVERS

You'd hardly expect me to make an instant diagnosis.

KEN

Did Dr. Emerson send you?

DR. TRAVERS
I work here, in the hospital.

KEN
Ah.

DR. TRAVERS
Would you describe yourself as suffering from paranoia?

KEN
No.

DR. TRAVERS
What would you say paranoia was?

KEN
Difficult. It depends on the person. A man whose feelings of security are tied to his own sense of what is right and can brook no denial. If he were, say, a sculptor, then we would describe his mental condition as paranoia. If, on the other hand, he was a doctor, we would describe it as professionalism.

DR. TRAVERS
(*Laughing*)
You don't like doctors!

KEN
Do you like patients?

DR. TRAVERS
Some.

KEN
I like some doctors.

DR. TRAVERS
What's wrong with doctors then?

KEN
Speaking generally, I suppose that as a profession
you've not learned that the level of awareness of the
population has risen dramatically; that black magic
is no longer much use and that people *can* and *want*
to understand what's wrong with them and many of
them can make decisions about their own lives.

DR. TRAVERS
What they need is information.

KEN
Of course, but as a rule, doctors dole out information
like a kosher butcher gives out pork sausages.

DR. TRAVERS
That's fair. But you'd agree that patients need medical knowledge to make good decisions?

KEN
I would. Look at me, for example. I'm a sculptor, an
airy-fairy artist, with no real hard knowledge and no
capability to understand anything about my body.
You're a doctor but I think I would hold my own
with a competition in anatomy with *you*.

DR. TRAVERS
It's a long time since I did any anatomy.

KEN

Of course. Whereas I was teaching it every day up to six months ago. It wouldn't be fair.

DR. TRAVERS

Your knowledge of anatomy may be excellent, but what's your neurology like, or your dermatology, endocrinology, urology and so on.

KEN

Lousy, and in so far as these bear on my case, I should be grateful for information so that I can make a proper decision. But it is my decision. If you came to my studio to buy something, and look at all my work, and you say: "I want that bronze" and I say to you: "Look, you don't know anything about sculpture. The proportion of that is all wrong, the texture is boring and it should have been made in wood anyway. You are having the marble!" You'd think I was nuts. If you were sensible you'd ask for my professional opinion but if you were a mature adult, you'd reserve the right to choose for yourself.

DR. TRAVERS

But we're not talking about a piece of sculpture to decorate a room, but about your life.

KEN

That's right, Doctor. *My* life.

DR. TRAVERS

But your obvious intelligence weakens your case. I'm not saying that you would find life easy but you

do have resources that an unintelligent person
doesn't have.

KEN

That sounds like Catch 22. If you're clever and sane
enough to put up an invincible case for suicide, it
demonstrates you ought not to die.
  (DR. TRAVERS *moves the stool near the bed*)
That's a disturbing tidiness compulsion you've got
there.

DR. TRAVERS

I was an only child; enough of me. Have you any
relationships outside the hospital? . . . You're not
married, I see.

KEN

No, thank God.

DR. TRAVERS

A girl friend?

KEN

A fiancée, actually. I asked her not to visit me any
more. About a fortnight ago.

DR. TRAVERS

She must have been upset.

KEN

Better that than a lifetime's sacrifice.

DR. TRAVERS

She wanted to . . . stay with you then?

KEN

Oh yes . . . Had it all worked out . . . But she's a young healthy woman. She wants babies—real ones. Not ones that never *will* learn to walk.

DR. TRAVERS

But if that's what she really wants.

KEN

Oh come on, Doctor. If that's what she really wants, there's plenty of other cripples who want help. I told her to go to release her, I hope, from the guilt she would feel if she did what she really wanted to.

DR. TRAVERS

That's very generous.

KEN

Balls. Really, Doctor, I did it for *me*. It would destroy *my* self-respect if I allowed myself to become the object with which people can safely exploit their masochist tendencies.

DR. TRAVERS

That's putting it very strongly.

KEN

Yes. Too strong. But you are beginning to sound like the chaplain. He was in here the other day. He seemed to think I should be quite happy to be God's chosen vessel into which people could pour their compassion . . . That it was all right being a cripple because it made other folk feel good when they helped me.

DR. TRAVERS
What about your parents?

KEN
Working class folk—they live in Scotland. I thought
it would break my mother—I always thought of my
father as a very tough egg. But it was the other way
round. My father can only think with his hands. He
used to stand around here—completely at a loss. My
mother would sit there—just understanding. She
knows what suffering's about. They were here a
week ago—I got rid of my father for a while and told
my mother what I was going to do. She looked at me
for a minute. There were tears in her eyes. She said:
"Aye lad, it's thy life . . . don't worry about your
dad—I'll get him over it" . . . She stood up and I
said: "What about you?" "What about me?" she
said, "Do you think life's so precious to me, I'm
frightened of dying?" . . . I'd like to think I was
my mother's son.

DR. TRAVERS
. . . Yes, well, we shall have to see . . .

KEN
What about? You mean you haven't made up your
mind?

DR. TRAVERS
. . . I shall have to do some tests . . .

KEN
What tests, for Christ's sake? I can tell you now, my
time over a hunderd meters is lousy.

DR. TRAVERS

You seem very angry.

KEN

Of course I'm angry . . . No, no . . . I'm . . . Yes.
I am angry.
(*Breathing*)
But I am trying to hold it in because you'll just write
me off as in a manic phase of a manic-depressive
cycle.

DR. TRAVERS

You are very free with psychiatric jargon.

KEN

Oh, well then, you'll be able to say I'm an obsessive
hypochondriac.
(*Breathing*)

DR. TRAVERS

I certainly wouldn't do that, Mr. Harrison.

KEN

Can't you see what a trap I am in? Can anyone prove
that they are sane? Could you?

DR. TRAVERS

. . . I'll come and see you again.

KEN

No, don't come and see me again, because every
time you come I'll get more and more angry, and
more and more upset and depressed. And eventu-
ally you will destroy my mind.

DR. TRAVERS

I'm sorry if I upset you, Mr. Harrison.
(DR. TRAVERS *replaces the stool and exits.
He crosses to the* SISTER's *office. Enter* DR.
SCOTT *and* MR. HILL)

DR. SCOTT

I hate the idea. It's against all my training and instincts . . .

HILL

Mine, too. But in this case, we're not dealing with
euthanasia, are we?

DR. SCOTT

Something very close.

HILL

No. Something very far away. Suicide.

DR. SCOTT

Thank you for a lovely meal.

HILL

Not at all; I am glad you accepted. Tell me, what
would you think, or rather feel, if there was a miracle and Ken Harrison was granted the use of his
arms for just one minute and he used them to grab a
bottle of sleeping tablets and swallowed the lot?

DR. SCOTT

. . . It's irrational but . . . I'd be very . . . re-
lieved.

HILL

It wouldn't go against your instincts? . . . You wouldn't feel it was a wasted life and fight with stomach pumps and all that?

DR. SCOTT

No . . . not if it was my decision.

HILL

You might even be sure there *was* a bottle of tablets handy and you not there.

DR. SCOTT

You make it harder and harder . . . but yes, I might do that . . . TonyMazza

HILL

Yes. Perhaps we ought to make suicide respectable again. Whenever anyone kills himself there's a whole legal rigmarole to go through—investigations, inquests and so on—and it all seems designed to find someone or something to *blame*. Can you ever recall a coroner saying something like: "We've heard all the evidence of how John Smith was facing literally insuperable odds and he made a courageous decision. I record a verdict of a noble death?"

DR. SCOTT

No . . . It's been a . . . very pleasant evening.

HILL

Thank you. For me too.

DR. SCOTT

I don't know if I've helped you though.

HILL

You have. I've made up my mind.

DR. SCOTT

You'll help him?

HILL

Yes . . . I hope you're not sorry.

DR. SCOTT

I'm pleased . . .

HILL

I'm sure it is morally wrong for anyone to try to hand
the responsibility for their death to anyone else.
And it's wrong to accept that responsibility, but Ken
isn't trying to do that.

DR. SCOTT

I'm glad you've made up your mind . . . Good
night.

(*They stop*)

HILL

I hope I see you again.

DR. SCOTT

I'm in the book . . . Goodnight.

HILL

Goodnight.

(They exit. NURSE SADLER goes into KEN's room with a meal)

KEN

You still on duty?

NURSE

We're very short-staffed . . .
   (She prepares to feed KEN with a spoon)
It looks good tonight . . . Minced beef.

KEN

Excellent . . . and what wine shall we order then?
How about a '48 claret. Yes, I think so . . . Send for
the wine waiter.

NURSE

You are a fool, Mr. Harrison.

KEN

Is there any reason why I shouldn't have wine?

NURSE

I don't know. I'll ask Sister if you like . . .

KEN

After all, the hospital seems determined to depress
my consciousness. But they'd probably think it's
immoral if I enjoy it.
   (NURSE SADLER gives him a spoonful of mince)
It's a bit salty.

NURSE

Do you want some water?

KEN

That would be good. Very nice . . . Not too full of
body. Château Ogston Reservoir, I think, with just a
cheeky little hint of Jeyes fluid from the sterilizer.

NURSE

We use Milton.

KEN

Oh dear . . . you'd better add to my notes. The final
catastrophe. Mr. Harrison's palate is failing; rush up
the emergency taste resuscitation unit.
       (In a phony American accent)
"Nurse, give me orange . . . No response . . .
Quick the lemon . . . God! Not a flicker . . . We're
on the tightrope . . . Nurse pass the ultimate . . .
Quick, there's no time to lose . . . Pass the hospital
mince." That would bring people back from the
dead. Don't tell Emerson that or he'll try it. I don't
want any more of that.
       (NURSE SADLER *exits*. DR. SCOTT *comes in*)

KEN

Sister.

DR. SCOTT

No, it's me. Still awake?

KEN

Yes.

DR. SCOTT

It's late.

KEN

What time is it?

DR. SCOTT

Half past eleven.

KEN

The Night Sister said I could have the light for half
an hour. I couldn't sleep. I wanted to think.

DR. SCOTT

Yes.

KEN

You look lovely.

DR. SCOTT

Thank you.

KEN

Have you been out?

DR. SCOTT

For a meal.

KEN

Nice. Good company?

DR. SCOTT

You're fishing.

KEN

That's right.

DR. SCOTT

Yes, it was good company.

KEN

A colleague?

DR. SCOTT

No. Actually it was Philip Hill, your solicitor.

KEN

Well, well, well . . . The randy old devil. He didn't
take long to get cracking, did he?

DR. SCOTT

It was just a dinner.

KEN

I know I engaged him to act for me. I didn't realize
he would see his duties so comprehensively.

DR. SCOTT

It was just a dinner!

KEN

Well, I hope my surrogate self behaved myself.

DR. SCOTT

You were a perfect gentleman.

KEN

Mm . . . then perhaps I'd better engage another
surrogate.

DR. SCOTT

Do you mind really?

KEN

. . . No. Unless you convinced him that Emerson
was right.

DR. SCOTT

. . . I didn't try.

KEN

Thank you.

DR. SCOTT

I think you are enjoying all this.

KEN

I suppose I am in a way. For the first time in six
months I feel like a human being again.

DR. SCOTT

Yes.

(*A pause*)

Isn't that the whole point Ken, that . . .

KEN

You called me Ken.

DR. SCOTT

Do you mind?

KEN

Oh! No, I liked it. I'll just chalk it up as another credit for today.

DR. SCOTT

I was saying, isn't that just the point; isn't that what this fight has shown you? That you are a human being again. You're not fighting for death. I don't think you want to win.

KEN

That was what I had to think about.

DR. SCOTT

And you have . . . Changed your mind?

KEN

. . . No. I know I'm enjoying the fight and I had to be sure that I wanted to win, really get what I'm fighting for, and not just doing it to convince myself I'm still alive.

DR. SCOTT

And are you sure?

KEN

Yes, quite sure; for me life is over. I want it recognized because I can't do the things that I want to do. That means I can't say the things I want to say. Is that a better end? You understand, don't you?

(NURSE SADLER *comes in with a feeding cup*)

NURSE

I didn't know you were here, Doctor.

DR. SCOTT

Yes, I'm just going.

KEN

See what I mean, Doctor. Here is my substitute mum, with her porcelain pap. This isn't for me.

DR. SCOTT

No . . .

KEN

So tomorrow, on with the fight!

DR. SCOTT

Goodnight . . . and good luck.

(FADE)

KERSHAW

So our psychiatrist is prepared to state that Harrison is sane.

HILL

Yes, he was sure. I'll have his written report tomorrow. He said he could understand the hospital fighting to save their patient from himself, but no matter how much he sympathized with them and how much he wished he could get Harrison to change his mind, nevertheless, he was sane and knew exactly what he was doing and why he was doing it.

KERSHAW

And you say that the hospital is holding him here under Section 26.

HILL

Yes, they rang me this morning. They got another chap in from Ellertree to sign it as well as Emerson.

KERSHAW

Hm . . . Tricky. There's no precedent for this, you know. Fascinating.

HILL

Yes.

KERSHAW

And you're sure in your mind he knows what he's doing?

HILL

Yes.

KERSHAW

. . . Well . . . Let's see him, shall we?

HILL

Here's the Sister's office.

KERSHAW

Is she your standard gorgon?

HILL

Only on the outside. But under that iron surface beats a heart of stainless steel.

(*They go into* SISTER's *office*)

HILL

Good morning, Sister.

SISTER

Morning, Mr. Hill.

HILL

This is a colleague, Mr. Kershaw.

SISTER

Good morning.

KERSHAW

Good morning.

HILL

Is it all right to see Mr. Harrison? . . .

SISTER

Have you asked Dr. Emerson?

HILL

Oh yes . . . before we came . . .

SISTER

I see . . .

HILL

You can check with him . . .

SISTER

. . . I don't think that's necessary . . . However, I'm afraid I shall have to ask you if I can stay with Mr. Harrison whilst you interview him.

HILL

Why?

SISTER

We are very worried about Mr. Harrison's mental condition as you know. Twice recently he has . . . got excited . . . and his breathing function has not been able to cope with the extra demands. Dr. Emerson has ordered that at any time Mr. Harrison is subjected to stress, someone must be there as a precaution.

HILL

. . . I see.
> (*He glances at* MR. KERSHAW, *who shrugs*)

Very well.

SISTER

This way, gentlemen.
> (*They go into* KEN's *room*)

HILL

Good morning, Mr. Harrison.

KEN

Morning.

HILL

I've brought along Mr. Kershaw. He is the barrister who is advising us.

KERSHAW

Good morning, Mr. Harrison.

HILL

Your doctor has insisted that Sister remains with us—to see you don't get too excited.

KEN

Oh! Sister, you know very well that your very presence always excites me tremendously. It must be the white apron and black stockings. A perfect mixture of mother and mistress.

(SISTER *grins a little sheepishly and takes a seat at the head of the bed.* KEN *strains his head to look at her.* SISTER *turns back the covers*)

Sister, what are you doing! Oh. Just for a minute there, Sister . . .

(SISTER *takes his pulse*)

HILL

. . . Well . . .

SISTER

Just a moment Mr. Hill . . .

(*She finishes taking the pulse*)

Very well.

KEN

So, Mr. Kershaw, what is your advice?

(MR. KERSHAW *pauses.* MR. HILL *makes to speak but* MR. KERSHAW *stops him with a barely perceptible shake of the head. A longer pause*)

KERSHAW

. . . If you succeed in your aim, you will be dead within a week.

KEN

I know.

KERSHAW

. . . I am informed that without a catheter the toxic substance will build up in your bloodstream and you will be slowly poisoned by your own blood.

KEN
(*Smiles*)

. . . You should have brought along a tape-recorder. That speech would be much more dramatic with sound effects!

KERSHAW
(*Relaxing and smiling*)

I had to be sure you know what you are doing.

KEN

I know.

KERSHAW

And you have no doubt whatsoever; no slightest reservations? . . .

KEN

None at all.

KERSHAW

Let's look at the possibilities. You are now being held under the Mental Health Act Section 26, which means they can keep you here and give you any treatment they believe you need. Under the law we can appeal to a tribunal.

KEN

How long will that take?

KERSHAW

. . . Up to a year.

KEN

A year! A year! Oh God, can't it be quicker than that?

KERSHAW

It might be quicker, but it could be a year.

KEN

Jesus Christ! I really would be crazy in a year.

KERSHAW

That's the procedure.

KEN

I couldn't stay like this for another year, I couldn't.

HILL

We could always try habeas corpus.

KERSHAW

That would depend if we could find someone.

KEN

Habeas corpus? What's that? I thought it was something to do with criminals.

KERSHAW

Well, it usually is, Mr. Harrison. Briefly, it's against the law to deprive anyone of their liberty without proper cause. If anyone is so deprived, they or a friend can apply for a writ of habeas corpus, which is the Latin for "you may have the body."

KEN

Particularly apt in my case.

KERSHAW

. . . The people who are doing the detaining have
to produce the . . . person, before the judge and if
they can't give a good enough reason for keeping
him, the judge will order that he be released.

KEN

It sounds as if it will take as long as that tribunal you
were talking about.

KERSHAW

No. Habeas corpus is one of the very few legal pro-
cesses that move very fast. We can approach any
judge at any time even when the courts aren't sitting
and he will see that it's heard straight away—in a
day or so usually.

HILL

If you could find a judge to hear it.

KEN

Why shouldn't a judge hear it?

KERSHAW

Habeas corpus itself is fairly rare. This would be
rarer.

KEN

Will I have to go to court?

KERSHAW

I doubt it. The hearing can be in court or in private,
in the Judge's Chambers as we say. The best thing

to do in this case is for Mr. Hill and I to find a judge, issue the writ, then I'll get together with the hospital's barrister and we'll approach the judge together and suggest we hold the subsequent hearing here.

KEN

In this room?

KERSHAW

I expect the judge will agree. If he ordered you to be produced in court and anything happened to you, it would be a classical case of prejudging the issue.

KEN

I wouldn't mind.

KERSHAW

But the judge would feel rather foolish. I should think it would be in a few days.

KEN

Thank you. It'll be an unusual case for you—making a plea for the defendant's death.

KERSHAW

I'll be honest with you. It's a case I could bear to lose.

KEN

If you do—it's a life sentence for me.

KERSHAW

Well, we shall see. Good morning, Mr. Harrison.
(*They go out with the* SISTER. *The pause at the* SISTER'*s office*)

HILL

Thank you very much, Sister . . . I'm very sorry about all this. I do realize it must be upsetting for you.

SISTER

Not at all, Mr. Hill. As I have a stainless steel heart, it's easy to keep it sterilized of emotion. Good morning.

(*She goes into her room.* HILL *and* KER-SHAW *go out*)

(*CROSS FADE on* KEN's *room*)

(JOHN *and* NURSE SADLER *are setting chairs for the hearing.* JOHN *begins to sing "Dry Bones"*)

NURSE

John!

JOHN

What's the matter?
(NURSE SADLER *is confused*)

NURSE

Nothing of course . . . silly . . .
(KEN *picks up the vibes between the two*)

KEN

Hello, hello . . . What have we here? Don't tell me that Cupid has donned his antiseptic gown and is flying the corridors of the hospital, shooting his hypodermic syringes into maidens' hearts . . .

NURSE

No!

KEN

John?

JOHN

Honestly, your honor, I'm not guilty. I was just walking down the corridor when I was struck dumb by the beauty of this nurse.

NURSE

Don't be an idiot, John . . . We need an extra chair . . . Can you go and find one please?

JOHN

Your wishes, oh queen, are my command.
(*He bows and goes out*)

NURSE

He is a fool.

KEN

He isn't. He's been bloody good to me. Have you been out with him? . . . It's none of my business, of course.

NURSE

We went to a club of his last night . . . He plays in a band, you know.

KEN

Yes, I know.

NURSE

They're really good. They should go a long
way . . . Still, I shouldn't be going on like this.

KEN

Why not? . . . Because I'm paralyzed? Because I
can't go dancing?

NURSE

Well . . .

KEN

The other day I was low and said to John, who was
shaving me, I was useless, what could I do? I served
no purpose and all the rest of the whining miseries.
John set about finding things I could do. He said,
first, because I could move my head from side to
side

(KEN *does so*)

I could be a tennis umpire; then as my head was
going, I could knock a pendulum from side to side
and keep a clock going. Then he said I could be a
child-minder and because kids were always doing
what they shouldn't I could be perpetually shaking
my head. He went on and on getting more and more
fantastic—like radar scanners. I laughed so much
that the Sister had to rush in and give me oxygen.

NURSE

He is funny.

KEN

He's more than that. He's free!

NURSE

Free?

KEN

Free of guilt. Most everybody here feels guilt about
me—including you. That's why you didn't want to
tell me what a fantastic time you had dancing. So
everybody makes me feel worse because I make
them feel guilty. But not John. He's sorry for me but
he knows bloody well it isn't his fault. He's a tonic.

(JOHN *comes back carrying* SISTER's
armchair)

NURSE

John! Did Sister say you could have that chair?

JOHN

She wasn't there . . .

NURSE

She'll kill you; no one ever sits in her chair.

JOHN

Why? Is it contaminated or something? I just
thought that if the poor old Judge had to sit here
listening to that miserable bugger moaning on about
wanting to die, the least we could do was to make
him comfortable.

KEN

(*Laughing to* NURSE SADLER)

See?

(JOHN *sits in the chair and assumes a grave
face*)

JOHN

Now, this is a very serious case. The two charges are
proved . . . Firstly, this hospital has been found
guilty of using drugs to make people happy. That's
terrible. Next and most surprising of all, this hospital, in spite of all their efforts to the contrary, are
keeping people alive! We can't have that.

(*Footsteps outside*)

NURSE

Sister's coming!
    (JOHN *jumps up and stands between the*
    chair and the door. SISTER *comes in and as*
    she approaches the bed with her back to
    the chair, JOHN *slips out of the room*)

KEN

Well now, we have some very important visitors today, Sister.

SISTER

Indeed we have.

KEN

Will you be here?

SISTER

No.

KEN

I feel a bit like a traitor.

SISTER

. . . We all do what we've got to.

KEN

That's right, but not all of us do it as well as you Sister . . .

SISTER
(*Rapidly*)

. . . Thank you.
(*She moves quickly to go.* DR. SCOTT *comes in*)

DR. SCOTT

Good morning, Sister.

SISTER
(*Brightly*)

Good morning.
(*She goes quickly without noticing the chair.* DR. SCOTT *watches her go*)

KEN

I've upset her, I'm afraid.

DR. SCOTT

You shouldn't do that. She is a marvelous Sister. You ought to see some of the others.

KEN

That's what I told her.

DR. SCOTT

Oh, I see. Well, I should think that's just about the one way past her defenses. How are you this morning?

KEN

Fine.

DR. SCOTT

And you're going ahead with it?

KEN

Of course.

DR. SCOTT

Of course.

KEN

I haven't had any tablets, yesterday or today.

DR. SCOTT

No.

KEN

Thank you.

DR. SCOTT

Thank the Judge. He ordered it.

KEN

Ah!

(DR. EMERSON *comes in*)

DR. EMERSON

Good morning, Mr. Harrison.

KEN

Morning, Doctor.

DR. EMERSON

There's still time.

KEN

No, I want to go on with it . . . unless you'll discharge me.

DR. EMERSON

I'm afraid I can't do that. The Judge and lawyers are conferring. I thought I'd just pop along and see if you were all right. We've made arrangements for the witnesses to wait in the Sister's office. I am one, so I should be grateful if you would remain here, with Mr. Harrison.

DR. SCOTT

Of course.

DR. EMERSON

Well, I don't want to meet the Judge before I have to. I wish you the best of luck, Mr. Harrison, so that we'll be able to carry on treating you.

KEN
(Smiling)

Thank you for your good wishes.
          (DR. EMERSON nods and goes out)

DR. SCOTT

If I didn't know *you* I'd say *he* was the most obstinate man I've ever met.
          (As DR. EMERSON makes for his office, MR.
          HILL comes down the corridor)

HILL

Good morning.

DR. EMERSON

Morning.

> (MR. HILL *stops and calls after* DR. EMER-
> SON)

HILL

Oh, Dr. Emerson . . .

DR. EMERSON

Yes?

HILL

I don't know . . . I just want to say how sorry I am
that you have been forced into such a . . . distaste-
ful situation.

DR. EMERSON

It's not over yet, Mr. Hill. I have every confidence
that the law is not such an ass that it will force me to
watch a patient of mine die unnecessarily.

HILL

We are just as confident that the law is not such an
ass that it will allow anyone arbitrary power.

DR. EMERSON

My power isn't arbitrary; I've earned it with knowledge and skill and it's also subject to the laws of
nature.

HILL

And to the laws of the state.

DR. EMERSON

If the state is so foolish as to believe it is competent
to judge a purely professional issue.

HILL

It's always doing that. Half the civil cases in the calendar arise because someone is challenging a professional's opinion.

DR. EMERSON

I don't know about other professions but I do know this one, medicine, is being seriously threatened because of the intervention of law. Patients are becoming so litigious that doctors will soon be afraid to offer any opinion or take any action at all.

HILL

Then they will be sued for negligence.

DR. EMERSON

We can't win.

HILL

Everybody wins. You wouldn't like to find yourself powerless in the hands of, say, a lawyer or a . . . bureaucrat. I wouldn't like to find myself powerless in the hands of a doctor.

DR. EMERSON

You make me sound as if I were some sort of Dracula . . .

HILL

No! . . . I for one certainly don't doubt your good faith but in spite of that I wouldn't like to place *anyone* above the law.

DR. EMERSON

I don't want to be above the law; I just want to be under laws that take full account of professional opinion.

HILL

I'm sure it will do that, Dr. Emerson. The question
is, whose professional opinion?

DR. EMERSON

We shall see.

> (MR. ANDREW EDEN, *the hospital's barris-
> ter, and* MR. HILL *and* MR. KERSHAW *come
> into* KEN's *room*)

HILL

Morning, Mr. Harrison. This is Mr. Eden who will
be representing the hospital.

KEN

Hello.

> (*They settle themselves into the chairs. The*
> SISTER *enters with the* JUDGE)

SISTER

Mr. Justice Millhouse.

JUDGE

Mr. Kenneth Harrison?

KEN

Yes, my Lord.

JUDGE

This is an informal hearing which I want to keep as
brief as possible. You are, I take it, Dr. Scott?

DR. SCOTT

Yes, my Lord.

JUDGE

I should be grateful, Doctor, if you would interrupt the proceedings at any time you think it necessary.

DR. SCOTT

Yes, my Lord.

JUDGE

I have decided in consultation with Mr. Kershaw and Mr. Hill that we shall proceed thus. I will hear a statement from Dr. Michael Emerson as to why he believes Mr. Harrison is legally detained, and then a statement from Dr. Richard Barr, who will support the application. We have decided not to subject Mr. Harrison to examination and cross-examination.

KEN

But I . . .

JUDGE
(*Sharply*)

Just a moment, Mr. Harrison. If, as appears likely, there remains genuine doubt as to the main issue, I shall question Mr. Harrison myself. Dr. Scott, I wonder if you would ask Dr. Emerson to come in.

DR. SCOTT

Yes, my Lord.
(*She goes out*)

Would you come in now, sir?
(SISTER *and* DR. EMERSON *come into* KEN's *room*)

JUDGE

Dr. Emerson, I would like you to take the oath.
(*The* JUDGE *hands* DR. EMERSON *a card with the oath written on it*)

DR. EMERSON
I swear the evidence that I give shall be the truth,
the whole truth and nothing but the truth.

JUDGE
Stand over there, please.
> (*The* JUDGE *nods to* MR. EDEN)

EDEN
You are Dr. Michael Emerson?

DR. EMERSON
I am.

EDEN
And what is your position here?

DR. EMERSON
I am a consultant physician and in charge of the
intensive care unit.

EDEN
Dr. Emerson, would you please give a brief account
of your treatment of this patient.

DR. EMERSON
(*Referring to notes*)
Mr. Harrison was admitted here on the afternoon of
October 9th, as an emergency following a road accident. He was suffering from a fractured left tibia
and right tibia and fibia, a fractured pelvis, four fractured ribs, one of which had punctured the lung,
and a dislocated fourth vertebra, which had ruptured the spinal cord. He was extensively bruised

and had minor lacerations. He was deeply unconscious and remained so for thirty hours. As a result
of treatment all the broken bones and ruptured tis-
sue have healed with the exception of a severed
spinal cord and this, together with a mental trauma,
is now all that remains of the initial injury.

EDEN

Precisely, Doctor. Let us deal with those last two
points. The spinal cord. Will there be any further
improvement in that?

DR. EMERSON

In the present state of medical knowledge, I would
think not.

EDEN

And the mental trauma you spoke of?

DR. EMERSON

It's impossible to injure the body to the extent that
Mr. Harrison did and not affect the mind. It is com-
mon in these cases that depression and the ten-
dency to make wrong decisions goes on for months,
even years.

EDEN

And in your view Mr. Harrison is suffering from
such a depression?

DR. EMERSON

Yes.

EDEN

Thank you, Doctor.

JUDGE

Mr. Kershaw?

KERSHAW

Doctor. Is there any objective way you could demonstrate this trauma? Are there, for example, the results of any tests, or any measurements you can take to show it to us?

DR. EMERSON

No.

KERSHAW

Then how do you distinguish between a medical syndrome and a sane, even justified, depression?

DR. EMERSON

By using my thirty years' experience as a physician, dealing with both types.

KERSHAW

No more questions, my Lord.

JUDGE

Mr. Eden, do you wish to re-examine?

EDEN

No, my Lord.

JUDGE

Thank you, Doctor. Would you ask Dr. Barr if he would step in please?
    (DR. EMERSON goes out)

DR. EMERSON

It's you now, Barr.
    (SISTER brings DR. BARR into KEN's room)

SISTER

Dr. Barr.

JUDGE

Dr. Barr, will you take the oath please.
                    (*He does so*)
Mr. Kershaw.

KERSHAW

You are Dr. Richard Barr?

DR. BARR

I am.

KERSHAW

And what position do you hold?

DR. BARR

I am a consultant psychiatrist at Norwood Park
Hospital.

KERSHAW

That is primarily a mental hospital is it not?

DR. BARR

It is.

KERSHAW

Then you must see a large number of patients suffering from depressive illness.

DR. BARR

I do, yes.

KERSHAW

You have examined Mr. Harrison?

DR. BARR

I have, yes.

KERSHAW

Would you say that he was suffering from such an
illness?

DR. BARR

No, I would not.

KERSHAW

Are you quite sure, Doctor?

DR. BARR

Yes, I am.

KERSHAW

The court has heard evidence that Mr. Harrison is
depressed. Would you dispute that?

DR. BARR

No, but depression is not necessarily an illness. I
would say that Mr. Harrison's depression is reactive
rather than endogenous. That is to say, he is react-
ing in a perfectly rational way to a very bad situation.

KERSHAW

Thank you, Dr. Barr.

JUDGE

Mr. Eden?

EDEN

Dr. Barr. Are there any objective results that you
could produce to prove Mr. Harrison is capable?

DR. BARR

There are clinical symptoms of endogenous depression, of course, disturbed sleep patterns, loss of appetite, lassitude, but, even if they were present, they would be masked by the physical condition.

EDEN

So how can you be sure this *is* in fact just a reactive depression?

DR. BARR

Just by experience, that's all, and by discovering when I talk to him that he has a remarkably incisive mind and is perfectly capable of understanding his position and of deciding what to do about it.

EDEN

One last thing, Doctor, do you think Mr. Harrison has made the right decision?

KERSHAW
(*Quickly*)

Is that really relevant, my Lord? After all . . .

JUDGE

Not really . . .

DR. BARR

I should like to answer it though.

JUDGE

Very well.

DR. BARR

No, I thought he made the wrong decision.
(*To* KEN)

Sorry.

EDEN
No more questions, my Lord.

JUDGE
Do you wish to re-examine, Mr. Kershaw?

KERSHAW
No, thank you, my Lord.

JUDGE
That will be all, Dr. Barr.
    (DR. BARR *goes out. The* JUDGE *stands*)

JUDGE
Do you feel like answering some questions?

KEN
Of course.

JUDGE
Thank you.

KEN
You are too kind.

JUDGE
Not at all.

KEN
I mean it. I'd prefer it if you were a hanging judge.

JUDGE
There aren't any any more.

KEN

Society is now much more sensitive and humane?

JUDGE

You could put it that way.

KEN

I'll settle for that.

JUDGE

I would like you to take the oath. Dr. Scott, his right
hand, please.

(KEN *takes the oath*)

The consultant physician here has given evidence
that you are not capable of making a rational decision.

KEN

He's wrong.

JUDGE

When then do you think he came to that opinion?

KEN

He's a good doctor and won't let a patient die if he
can help it.

JUDGE

He found that you were suffering from acute depression.

KEN

Is that surprising? I am almost totally paralyzed. I'd
be insane if I *weren't* depressed.

JUDGE

But there is a difference between being unhappy and being depressed in the medical sense.

KEN

I would have thought that my psychiatrist answered that point.

JUDGE

But, surely, wishing to die must be strong evidence that the depression has moved beyond a mere unhappiness into a medical realm?

KEN

I don't wish to die.

JUDGE

Then what is this case all about?

KEN

Nor do I wish to live at any price. Of course I want to live, but as far as I am concerned I'm dead already. I merely require the doctors to recognize the fact. I cannot accept this condition constitutes life in any real sense at all.

JUDGE

Certainly, you're alive legally.

KEN

I think I could challenge even that.

JUDGE

How?

KEN

Any reasonable definition of life must include the idea of its being self-supporting. I seem to remember something in the papers—when all the heart transplant controversy was on—about it being all right to take someone's heart if they require constant attention from respirators and so on to keep them alive.

JUDGE

There also has to be absolutely no brain activity at all. Yours is certainly working.

KEN

It is and sanely.

JUDGE

That is the question to be decided.

KEN

My Lord, I am not asking anyone to kill me. I am only asking to be discharged from this hospital.

JUDGE

It comes to the same thing.

KEN

Then that proves my point; not just the fact that I will spend the rest of my life in hospital, but that whilst I am here, everything is geared just to keeping my brain active, with no real possibility of it ever being able to direct anything. As far as I can see, that is an act of deliberate cruelty.

JUDGE

Surely, it would be more cruel if society let people die, when it could, with some effort, keep them alive.

KEN

No, not *more* cruel, *just* as cruel.

JUDGE

Then why should the hospital let you die—if it is just as cruel?

KEN

The cruelty doesn't reside in saving someone or allowing them to die. It resides in the fact that the choice is removed from the man concerned.

JUDGE

But a man who is very desperately depressed is not capable of making a reasonable choice.

KEN

As you said, my Lord, that is the question to be decided.

JUDGE

All right. You tell me why it is a reasonable choice that you decided to die.

KEN

It is a question of dignity. Look at me here. I can do nothing, not even the basic primitive functions. I cannot even urinate, I have a permanent catheter attached to me. Every few days my bowels are washed out. Every few hours two nurses have to turn me over or I would rot away from bedsores. Only my brain functions unimpaired but even that is futile because I can't act on any conclusions it comes to. This hearing proves that. Will you please listen.

JUDGE

I am listening.

KEN

I choose to acknowledge the fact that I am in fact dead and I find the hospital's persistent effort to maintain this shadow of life an indignity and it's inhumane.

JUDGE

But wouldn't you agree that many people with appalling physical handicaps have overcome them and lived essentially creative, dignified lives?

KEN

Yes, I would, but the dignity starts with their choice. If I choose to live, it would be appalling if society killed me. If I choose to die, it is equally appalling if society keeps me alive.

JUDGE

I cannot accept that it is undignified for society to devote resources to keeping someone alive. Surely it enhances that society.

KEN

It is not undignified if the man wants to stay alive,
but I must restate that the dignity starts with his
choice. Without it, it is degrading because technol-
ogy has taken over from human will. My Lord, if I
cannot be a man, I do not wish to be a medical
achievement. I'm fine . . . I am fine.

JUDGE

It's all right. I have no more questions.
(*The* JUDGE *stands up and walks to the
window. He thinks a moment*)

JUDGE

This is a most unusual case. Before I make a judg-
ment I want to state that I believe all the parties
have acted in good faith. I propose to consider this
for a moment. The law on this is fairly clear. A deliberate decision to embark on a course of action
that will lead inevitably to death is not *ipso facto*
evidence of insanity. If it were, society would have
to reward many men with a dishonorable burial
rather than a posthumous medal for gallantry. On
the other hand, we do have to bear in mind that Mr.
Harrison has suffered massive physical injuries and
it is possible that his mind is affected. Any judge in
his career will have met men who are without doubt
insane in the meaning of the Act and yet appear in
the witness box to be rational. We must, in this case,
be most careful not to allow Mr. Harrison's obvious
wit and intelligence to blind us to the fact that he
could be suffering from a depressive illness . . .

and so we have to face the disturbing fact of the
divided evidence . . . and bear in mind that, however much we may sympathize with Mr. Harrison in
his cogently argued case to be allowed to die, the
law instructs us to ignore it if it is the product of a
disturbed or clinically depressed mind . . . However, I am satisfied that Mr. Harrision is a brave and
cool man who is in complete control of his mental
faculties and I shall therefore make an order for him
to be set free.
>   (*A pause. The* JUDGE *walks over to* KEN)
Well, you got your hanging judge!

KEN

I think not, my Lord. Thank you.
>   (*The* JUDGE *nods and smiles*)

JUDGE

Goodbye.
>   (*He turns and goes. He meets* DR. EMERSON
>   *in the* SISTER'S *room. While he talks to
>   him, everyone else, except* DR. SCOTT,
>   *comes out*)
Ah, Dr. Emerson.

DR. EMERSON

My Lord?

JUDGE

I'm afraid you'll have to release your patient.

DR. EMERSON

I see.

JUDGE

I'm sorry. I understand how you must feel.

DR. EMERSON

Thank you.

JUDGE

If ever I have to have a road accident, I hope it's in this town and I finish up here.

DR. EMERSON

Thank you again.

JUDGE-

Goodbye.
> (*He walks down the corridor.* DR. EMERSON *stands a moment, then slowly goes back to the room.* KEN *is looking out of the window.* DR. SCOTT *is sitting by the bed*)

DR. EMERSON

Where will you go?

KEN

I'll get a room somewhere.

DR. EMERSON

There's no need.

KEN

Don't let's . . .

DR. EMERSON

We'll stop treatment, remove the drips. Stop feeding you if you like. You'll be unconscious in three days, dead in six at most.

KEN

There'll be no last minute resuscitation?

DR. EMERSON

Only with your express permission.

KEN

That's very kind; why are you doing it?

DR. EMERSON

Simple! You might change your mind.
> (KEN *smiles and shakes his head*)

KEN

Thanks. I won't change my mind, but I'd like to stay.
> (DR. EMERSON *nods and goes.* DR. SCOTT *stands and moves to the door. She turns and moves to* KEN *as if to kiss him*)

KEN

Oh, don't, but thank you.
> (DR. SCOTT *smiles weakly and goes out*)

> (*The lights are held for a long moment and then snap out*)

◢ BARD BOOKS

the classics, poetry, drama and distinguished modern fiction

FICTION

ANAIS NIN READER Ed., Philip K. Jason	49890	2.95
ANYA Susan Fromberg-Schaffer	48645	2.95
THE AWAKENING Kate Chopin	50948	2.50
BETRAYED BY RITA HAYWORTH Manuel Puig	36020	2.25
BEYOND THE BEDROOM WALL Larry Woiwode	47670	2.95
BILLIARDS AT HALF-PAST NINE Heinrich Böll	51383	2.95
BLANCO & THINGS ABOUT TO DISAPPEAR Allen Wier	49114	3.50
CALL IT SLEEP Henry Roth	49304	2.50
A SINGLE MAN Christopher Isherwood	37689	1.95
CATALOGUE George Milburn	33084	1.95
THE CLOWN Heinrich Böll	37523	2.25
DOM CASMURRO Machado De Assis	49668	2.95
EDWIN MULLHOUSE Steven Millhauser	37952	2.50
THE EIGHTH DAY Thornton Wilder	44149	2.95
THE EYE OF THE HEART Barbara Howes, Ed.	47787	2.95
GABRIELA, CLOVE AND CINNAMON Jorge Amado	51839	3.95
THE GALLERY John Horne Burns	33357	2.25
THE GREEN HOUSE Mario Vargas Liosa	42747	2.75
GROUP PORTRAIT WITH LADY Heinrich Böll	48637	2.50
HOPSCOTCH Julio Cortázar	36731	2.95
HUNGER Knut Hamsun	42028	2.25
HOUSE OF ALL NATIONS Christina Stead	18895	2.45

THE LAST DAYS OF LOUISIANA RED		
Ishmael Reed	35451	2.25
LESBIAN BODY Monique Wittig	31062	1.75
THE LIFE TO COME AND OTHER STORIES		
E. M. Forster	48611	2.95
THE LITTLE HOTEL Christina Stead	48389	2.50
A LONG AND HAPPY LIFE Reynolds Price	48132	2.25
THE LOST STEPS Alejo Carpentier	46177	2.50
LOVE STORIES BY NEW WOMEN		
Charleen Swansea and		
Barbara Campbell, Eds.	48058	2.75
LUCIFER WITH A BOOK		
John Horne Burns	33340	2.25
THE MAN WHO LOVED CHILDREN		
Christina Stead	40618	2.50
THE MAZE MAKER Michael Ayrton	23648	1.65
A MEETING BY THE RIVER		
Christopher Isherwood	37945	1.95
MYSTERIES Knut Hamsun	25221	1.95
NABOKOV'S DOZEN Vladimir Nabokov	15354	1.65
NIGHT Elie Wiesel	46797	2.25
NIGHT BOOK William Kotzwinkle	49106	2.50
ONE HUNDRED YEARS OF SOLITUDE		
Gabriel García Márquez	45278	2.95
PNIN Vladimir Nabokov	50906	2.50
PRATER VIOLET Christopher Isherwood	36269	1.95
REAL PEOPLE Alison Lurie	23747	1.65
THE RECOGNITIONS William Gaddis	49544	3.95
A ROSE IN THE HEART Edna O'Brien	50021	2.75
THE STORY OF HAROLD Terry Andrews	49965	2.95
STUDS LONIGAN TRILOGY		
James T. Farrell	31955	2.75
SUN CITY Tove Jansson	32318	1.95
SWEET ADVERSITY Donald Newlove	38364	2.95
THE TARTAR STEPPE Dino Buzzati	50252	2.75
TENT OF MIRACLES Jorge Amado	41020	2.75
THREE BY HANDKE Peter Handke	32458	2.25
THE TWO DEATHS OF QUINCAS		
WATERYELL Jorge Amado	50047	2.50
THE VIOLENT LAND Jorge Amado	47696	2.75
YIDDISH STORIES OLD AND NEW Edited		
by Irving Howe and Eliezer Greenberg	47803	2.50

Where better paperbacks are sold, or directly from the publisher. Include 50¢ per copy for postage and handling, allow 4-6 weeks for delivery.

Avon Books, Mail Order Dept.

224 West 57th Street, New York, N.Y. 10019

BD (2) 6-80